How to Create HIGH IMPACT Business Presentations

Joyce Kupsh   Pat R. Graves

Printed on recyclable paper

NTC Business Books

a division of *NTC Publishing Group* • Lincolnwood, Illinois USA

Library of Congress Cataloging-in-Publication Data

Kupsh, Joyce.
    How to create high-impact business presentations / Joyce Kupsh,
Pat R. Graves.
        p.   cm.
    Includes index.
    1. Business presentations.   2. Business presentations—Audio
-visual aids.   I. Graves, Pat R.   II. Title.
HF5718.22.K86   1992
658.4'5—dc20

1994 Printing

Published by NTC Business Books, a division of NTC Publishing Group
4255 West Touhy Avenue
Lincolnwood (Chicago), Illinois 60646-1975, U.S.A.

    4 5 6 7 8 9 BC 9 8 7 6 5 4 3 2

Foreword

The information explosion has placed a premium on effective communication–getting the right information in front of the right people at the right time and in the right format. Nowhere in organizations is effective communication so important as in the meeting room, one of the last frontiers of productivity improvement.

Increasingly, effective business communication will rely on visual presentations–diagrams, graphs, maps, photographs, animation, videos, replicas. Studies have shown that visuals boost audience retention and learning, heighten interest and enjoyment, and significantly influence meeting outcomes. Why? A picture or symbol conveys a whole idea, while spoken or printed words break an idea into pieces. Moreover, since half the brain consists of a powerful vision computer system, the mind processes visual information more efficiently. Consequently, well-designed visual presentations enable viewers to assimilate masses of data quickly and better understand complex relationships.

Visual images work best when the presenter carefully thinks through preparation, delivery, and follow-up. If visuals are added to a written speech as an afterthought or as decoration the effort is wasted. Authors Joyce Kupsh and Pat Graves explain how to conceive visuals in the early stages when planning a presentation strategy and developing a message. They describe the wide choice of media available, noting technological advances such as

LCD projection panels, computer-based slide shows, and multimedia. For the presenter who protests "I'm not an artist," the authors point to easy-to-use presentation software that offers graphic templates and libraries of clip art. The guidelines on using color explain how to evoke a theme or set a mood.

Equally important, the authors give practical advice on how to arrange the meeting room, conduct a meeting, and use presentation equipment. They offer a materials and equipment checklist as well as a sample evaluation form. Presenters who take these suggestions to heart will not only enhance their image in the minds of the audience but also feel more confident and self-assured. Having visuals guide the flow of the presentation frees a speaker from memorizing words or depending on note cards.

Every working day, millions of men and women place their personal and professional lives on the line as they stand up to make a business presentation. This book provides a comprehensive guide for anyone who suffers a tinge of stage fright when called to the front of the room.

Virginia Johnson
Manager
3M Meeting Management Institute

Table of Contents

Acknowledgments

We are very grateful to all those who have contributed to the book, especially our Graphic Design Consultant, Babette Mayor. Individually we would like to recognize the following people:

I would like to give special recognition to Paul Kupsh, Kristin Dee Carter, Jerry Kupsh, Brian Dietrich, and Roxy for all their loyal support and assistance. In addition, I want to thank my many graduate and undergraduate students who have used our materials and given me ideas for the book. Special recognition goes to Tanya Beck, Mary Buck, Angelique Rodriguez, and Carl Sandvik for their contributions.

Joyce Kupsh

I would like to recognize Susan Poduch, Denise Gillespie, and Elizabeth Martin for their contributions, along with my many other graduate and undergraduate students who used our materials and contributed ideas.

Pat R. Graves

Creating Effective Presentations

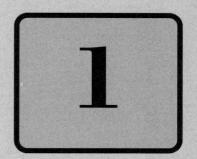

S^o . . . you have been asked to

- ✔ give a speech
- ✔ make a presentation
- ✔ say a few words
- ✔ provide some insight
- ✔ give a paper
- ✔ prepare a talk
- ✔ narrate a panel
- ✔ lead a group
- ✔ preside over a meeting

Whatever words are used, you are to be in front of people and are expected to perform. If you dread the experience, you may have one or more of the following symptoms: your hands sweat, your knees shake, your throat dries, and your heart pounds.

There is a fix for these symptoms. Although it may not prove to be a quick cure, it is a lasting one that will provide many rewards for you. You may still feel tension, but it will result from excitement and anticipation rather than dread.

This book contains the remedies for turning what might be a dreaded event into a thrilling opportunity. You will still be the "star" on the main stage, but you will be surrounded by a supporting cast–your visuals.

This chapter is designed to introduce you to the importance of business presentations; explain ways the image makes the difference; describe the advantages of using visuals; take a brief look at technology and high-impact presentations; and see how to get started.

You will be so ready you can hardly wait for opening night. You will be prepared and organized– and your presentation will have impact!

The Importance of Presentations

Presentations are an important communication medium in businesses, associations, and educational settings. They provide an opportunity to share a great deal of information in a very short time. Sources vary on how many presentations are given every day–some estimate 25 to 33 million. Individuals from every walk of life find they are being called upon to share information with others in a group. And, yet, few have been empowered with an inborn ability to be an effective speaker.

Presentations are a crucial part of meetings, and an effective presentation will have an impact on the success of meeting outcomes. While some studies confirm that the average business executive spends more than 50 percent of a typical day in meetings, often meetings are not the most stimulating events you can attend. In an editorial in *Presentation Products Magazine,* Lindstrom (November, 1990) made the following comment:

> Is there anyone who has not at some time attended a seminar, business meeting, or training session in which the stimuli were so light they could barely be detected? In a study of 200 U.S. corporate vice presidents by Motivational Systems in West Orange, New Jersey, 4 out of 10 of the executives admitted they have dozed off while listening to a presentation. When asked to

> Approximately 25 to 33 million presentations are made every day.

> High-impact presentations can reduce or eliminate boredom at meetings.

rate the average business presentation, 51.5 percent of the subjects said "interesting or stimulating," while 44.5 percent said "boring or unbearable." (The remaining four percent nodded off during the survey, I assume.)

3M, a leading supplier of presentation equipment and supplies for many years, recognized the need to improve meeting effectiveness by establishing a Meeting Management Institute (MMI). The MMI advisory board sets policies and guidelines for the institute and provides direction for its sponsorship of studies investigating how meetings can be improved to achieve greater results.

If presenters and meeting leaders can become more effective, personal and company productivity should increase. In today's competitive world, increased productivity is vital. The persuasive power of a high-impact presentation can be what makes the difference in your success.

> Increasing productivity is vital in today's competitive world.

This book will provide you with a basis for improving your presentations and, consequently, your effectiveness and productivity. You will create high-impact presentations that do make a difference.

The Image Makes the Difference

Presentations have one or more objectives: to inform, teach, motivate, or persuade. In fact, almost anything you wish to communicate in the form of a presentation will have some element of persuasion in it. If you want your audience to accept you and the ideas you share, you need to be prepared–both personally and professionally–so the image you create will get the results you want. Your appearance, attitude, and mannerisms are all important to form a good first impression. Today's presentation technology can help you increase your confidence and your level of preparedness by allowing you to develop and use well-designed visuals.

You, as a presenter, have the opportunity to improve the image you wish to project to an audience.

Appearance

An audience will immediately begin to form an impression of you the moment you enter the room. While many aspects of physical makeup cannot be changed, the style of clothes you wear will contribute to your image. For instance, does your attire fit in with an art deco crowd, or the business image of the nineties? Suits are still the norm, but more color is shown in women's business attire today.

Think about the formalness of the presentation situation when you select the clothes you wear. Think about how your audience might dress. If in doubt about your attire, be conservative.

Your grooming and physical hygiene reflect how you feel about yourself. Be sure you reflect a caring, "together," image.

Attitude

Your enthusiasm and positive attitude will be contagious. If you lack enthusiasm, you cannot expect your audience to readily accept your ideas and be enthusiastic. The image you project will suffer.

Mannerisms

Mannerisms should show you are decisive and in control. The audience should see your assurance. If you are uncertain of yourself, nervous mannerisms will give away your lack of self confidence.

Preparedness

Being prepared is a way of winning an audience and influencing their decisions. After all, if you have done your homework, you stand a much better chance of being able to influence them into your way of thinking.

Confidence

Confidence shows an audience that you believe in yourself and whatever it is you are representing to them. You must have confidence and good self-esteem (or give the image that you do) to gain the confidence of the audience.

Visuals

The visuals or audio-visual media you use in your presentations will also contribute to your image. They will help the audience form an opinion of your personal characteristics and credibility. Their *appearance* can project a favorable and impressive image. Visuals can also help you display enthusiasm by including real-life or drawn images to project the type of *attitude* you desire. By using visuals, you may find that your nervous mannerisms may disappear because the audience's attention will be diverted periodically as you speak. However, you do have the responsibility to learn and follow good audio-visual techniques in using them.

When you use well-prepared visuals, your *confidence* level improves. Instead of nervously holding notes or cards, your visuals can provide an outline for you as well as your audience. The time you spend organizing your thoughts and developing your visuals increases your *preparedness*.

Actually, if you accidentally lost your visuals on the way to the presentation, chances are you would still give a better presentation because of the organization and planning required to develop the visuals. This extra work undoubtedly gives you more familiarity with and confidence about the subject on which you are presenting.

Therefore, the image makes a difference in a variety of different ways. Bobbie Gee, a Laguna Beach management consultant, believes that a positive image and reputation are the most important assets an individual or company can possess. According to Gee, "an image can be whatever you want to make it."

The Advantages of Visuals

By designing visuals of some type to support your ideas, you will be required to prepare and organize your presentation. You will not depend on a stack of note cards or be compelled to memorize exact words. Your visuals will prompt and support you.

Using media to support your presentation and help your audience visualize has several distinct advantages which have been proven by research. When visuals are used, (1) retention and learning are

The power of visuals has been well-recognized since cavemen drew pictures on walls. Edgar Wycoff (April, 1977) said one of the first documented cases in the formal use of a visual aid occurred in Greece in the fourth century B.C. The great orator Hyperedies served as a lawyer for Phyrne, a young lady of "easy virtue and questionable reputation." As a rather hostile panel of judges was about to pronounce a severe judgment against his somewhat homely client, Hyperedies disrobed her in front of the court and commenced to plead for the preservation of one so beautiful.

increased; (2) meeting or class effectiveness is increased; and (3) the image of the speaker is enhanced.

Retention and Learning

An accepted learning principle is that people learn by doing. A trainer or teacher may wonder if visualization is an effective means of instruction. This theory was proven many years back by numerous research results showing that people can improve their learning of even a muscular response by merely sitting and looking and listening. Here is one of those studies:

> Subjects were first tested for skills like dart throwing, basketball foul shooting, and high jumping. These subjects were then asked to refrain from any physical practice and to sit quietly for five-minute periods daily for two weeks and to imagine themselves performing these exercises with some thought to improvement. On all three types of tasks, significant improvement was attained with no actual performance and no reinforcement by anyone (Bugelski, 1971).

Many research studies in a variety of subject areas have demonstrated how visuals make a difference in how people absorb information. A few of the studies that validate the effectiveness of using visuals include:

✔ Green (1984) quoted the following findings supporting the use of audio-visual presentations. Physiologically, 83 percent of all learning begins through the eyes. The Armed Forces have proven that people retain facts up to 55 percent longer when they learn by a combination of sight and sound.

> You can improve a skill by thinking–as well as by practicing.

> By seeing and hearing, people retain facts longer.

✔ Colthran (1989) cited two additional studies that prove the value of visuals. At the University of Wisconsin, researchers determined that learning improved up to 200 percent when visual aids were used in teaching vocabulary. Studies at Harvard and Columbia found audio-visuals improved retention from 14 to 38 percent over presentations where no visuals were used.

> Using visual aids improves both learning and retention.

✔ Kupsh (1975) proved the effectiveness of using synchronized sound-slide packages in teaching beginning typing. The experimental study showed that the use of five packages, each ten minutes or less in length, increased the knowledge of basic typing fundamentals during a semester course of beginning typing. In addition, students using the sound-slide packages reacted more favorably toward the class in an opinionnaire inventory.

> Media not only helps the students learn better, but also prompts them to enjoy class more.

Meeting Effectiveness

Many characteristics impact on meeting effectiveness. While this topic is discussed in greater detail in Chapter 10, consider how the use of visuals can influence the results of a meeting.

A study by the Wharton Applied Research Center of the Wharton School of Business showed that a simple overhead projector could significantly influence the outcome of a business meeting. Projector use reduced the length of the meeting by nearly one-third and also sparked a larger percentage of participants (nearly two-thirds) to make immediate decisions after the meeting (Oppenheim, 1981).

> Overhead projector use can reduce meeting length and promote immediate decisions.

Speaker Image

The same Wharton Study also found that presenters who used overhead projectors were rated more favorably overall (Oppenheim, 1981). Additional research at the University of Minnesota also found several interesting facts concerning how the use of visuals enhance a speaker's image.

> Both inexperienced and experienced speakers can benefit by using visuals.

✔ Use of overhead transparencies results in the presenter being perceived as more interesting but less professional than a presenter using 35 mm slides.

✔ Effectiveness varies as a function of speaker quality. A "typical" speaker using presentation support has nothing to lose and can be as effective as the better speaker who has used no visuals. The better the speaker is, the greater the need to use high-quality visual aids (Vogel, Dickson, Lehman, Shuart, 1986).

Technology and High-Impact Presentations

Times have changed! Centuries ago, speakers had the help of a megaphone to project their voices to a gathering of people, or they could draw pictures in the sand or on a stone. Until a few years ago, speakers operated in a relatively similar manner. If their voices needed amplification, they used microphones to project their voices instead of a megaphone. If they wanted to share a written message, they used a blackboard; or they provided typewritten handouts for the audience to take home.

Modern technology has provided new ways to communicate. The microphone is still useful and may be needed, but you no longer need to write on a blackboard. Today, speakers are presenters who have at their disposal a vast array of up-to-date tools.

Changes

Technology has opened the door for a variety of changes in both preparing and delivering presentations for meetings and training. Computer-generated visuals are now possible using a variety of software programs.

Technological equipment, including color printers and copiers, scanners, film recorders, optical disks, LCD panels, and video/data projectors, is being used to design and deliver presentations for meetings as well as training. Multimedia presentations integrate text and graphics, color, sound, animation, video, and interactivity to communicate information, express imagination, and gain audience involvement.

Changing to new methods made possible by technology can be a challenge. Yet, benefits such as improved quality and productivity are important. The competitive advantage may be what provides you the nudge to get started.

Learning new things may be thrilling, frightening, and time consuming all at once. Since using new technology requires a learning curve, productivity may initially be decreased rather than increased. However, at the end of the learning curve, your persistence will be rewarded.

Terminology

Are you giving a speech, making a presentation, or reading a paper? The authors assume these terms are synonymous and use them interchangeably. You may find your company or a professional organization using a particular set of terms.

Confusion may exist with the use of technological terms, also. As new developments occur, new words are coined. Similar to common words, these words may have different meanings for different people. A glossary is included at the end of the book, and new technology and presentation terminology is explained throughout the book. However, a basic overview of seven key terms is given at this point to help you establish a frame of reference.

Desktop. In the past, publication work was sent to others–either in-house or outside of the company–to complete. For instance, in producing a brochure, copy was sent to a typesetter and printer. Today, both the typesetting and the printing can be accomplished right at a computer workstation or *on the desktop.* Thus, the term desktop has evolved–even though in reality some work may still be sent out to specialists.

Desktop Publishing. Desktop publishing is changing expectations of the printed page. With today's hardware and software, appealing documents can be produced on your computer–*from the desktop*–using many of the techniques and capabilities which, just a few years ago, required typesetting and professional printing.

Actually, you can desktop publish with a word-processing computer program, but specialized desktop-publishing page layout software and a laser printer allow you to develop a more sophisticated layout and design. This software enables the user to perform or more easily accomplish tasks such as

✔ using different fonts, styles, and sizes
✔ setting up newspaper-type columns

Amy Ecclesine, editor of *Publish* (December, 1990), remarked that, in calculating the magazine's production record, the average is about eight people-hours for each square inch of published editorial text. Since the staff uses a very modern array of the latest hardware and software technology, you might question whether it took that long to produce a magazine in the past. But compare the quality, quantity, and timeliness of magazines today with those of 5, 10, or 20 years ago. Competition, or "keeping up with the Joneses," is not only nice but necessary in today's world.

✔ inserting lines and boxes

✔ using shading

✔ importing (bringing in) clip art, pictures, or work from other programs

Desktop Presentation. Desktop-presentation software is an even newer application. This software is used for the creation and display of presentation visuals. Specialized features of such programs include

✔ automatic sizing for slides, overheads, or computer-based screen shows

✔ word processing capabilities

✔ drawing features

✔ creating graphs

✔ importing clip art, pictures, or work from other programs

✔ running of computer-based screen shows

✔ creating miniatures for handouts and notes

Presentation Graphics. Presentation graphics is another term frequently found in computer literature. Some writers in the field consider it synonymous with desktop presentations. Others use the term more specifically to represent programs that create charts and graphs.

Graphics and Graphs. Graphics can be interpreted in several ways. For discussion purposes, this book considers graphics as image enhancements—such as lines, boxes, backgrounds, art, clip art, scanned images, photographs, etc. Graphs, on the other hand, refer specifically to numerical types of charts such as a

> You may wonder what a desktop presentation package can do that your word processing program cannot do. In general, a desktop presentation package makes the task a lot easier and quicker. See Appendix B for a list of presentation software.

pie or bar chart. More details on graphics and graphs are given in later chapters.

Presentation Media. Presentation media is a more broad term coined by Apple Computer, Inc., to encompass both the areas of desktop publishing and desktop presentations. This term makes a lot of sense. After all, a written report is a presentation on paper, and a slide show is a visual presentation. Both media present information. Thus, presentation media is used in this book as a general term including both the written format and the projected images.

Computer-Based Shows. Computer-based shows (also called slide, screen, or electronic shows), eliminate the need for making 35 mm slides or overhead transparencies by projecting the images directly on either a large monitor or on a projection screen. Although projecting your images in this way is exciting and has many benefits, the challenges of having the necessary equipment at the location of your presentation can be a problem. As equipment becomes more prevalent and less expensive, computer-based shows will become more common because of their many advantages.

Getting Started

You may not have the latest or most appropriate hardware and software for preparing your presentation. You also may not have the ideal facility in which to give your presentation. On the other hand, you may be able to select your preparation materials and equipment and have the opportunity to choose and set up your environment exactly as you desire. Therefore, this book contains information on the ideal situation and provides hints for dealing with situations that are not the ideal ones.

Since presentations are so diverse, a variety of scenarios and examples are used throughout the book. At one point, the book may use a situation where you are conducting a training seminar within your own company facility. In another, you may be arriving at a convention hotel as one of a hundred speakers to present on a program. Hopefully, you will relate with one or more of these situations. By reading and putting into practice the material in this book, you will find yourself a polished presenter frequently asked to speak.

References

Bugelski, B. R. (1971). *The Psychology of Learning Applied to Teaching.* Indianapolis: Bobbs-Merrill Company, Inc., 135-136.

Cothran, Tom. (July, 1989). "The Value of Visuals." *Presentation Technologies*, (Supplement to *Training*), 6.

Ecclesine, Amy. (December, 1990). "Editors' Forum." *Publish*, 12.

Green, Ronald E. (October, 1984). "The Persuasive Properties of Color." *Marketing Communications,* 50-54.

Kupsh, Joyce. (1975). "The Effectiveness of Synchronized Sound-Slide Packages in Beginning Typing." Unpublished doctoral dissertation, Arizona State University, Tempe.

Lindstrom, Robert. (November, 1990). "Podium." *Presentation Products Magazine*, 8.

Oppenheim, Lynn. (1981). *Study of the Effects of the Use of Overhead Transparencies on Business Meetings.* Philadelphia: Wharton Applied Research Center, Wharton School, University of Pennsylvania.

Vogel, Douglas R.; Dickson, Gary W.; Lehman, John; and Shuart, Kent. (1986). *Persuasion and the Role of Visual Presentation Support: The UM/3M Study.* Minneapolis: Management Information Systems Research Center, School of Management, University of Minnesota.

Wycoff, Edgar. (April, 1977). "Why Visuals." *Audio-Visual Communication*, 39.

Planning the Strategy

2

A presentation strategy is vital for making an effective presentation! Planning the presentation strategy involves analyzing your audience, considering your time element, investigating your resources, establishing your objectives, conducting your research, and checking your organization.

The emphasis of this chapter is on planning the presentation strategy. Considerations examined are the audience; the timeframe before and during the presentation; the resources available; the objectives; the research required; and the general organization of the presentation.

Analyze Your Audience

Every audience has a personality of its own. A speaker needs to assess the background, characteristics, and environment of every audience. Many questions should be asked to anticipate the needs and desires of the audience.

Background

If you are speaking to colleagues, you may already know a lot about their background. However, additional research may provide knowledge that can be helpful. In planning for a presentation outside your immediate organization, you may need to research and find the answers to many questions. These questions may vary with each audience.

For instance, to learn about the educational background of the audience, you could ask questions to find background information such as

✔ amount of education
✔ type of certificates or degrees received
✔ specialization areas or majors
✔ type and location of institutions attended

Next, you may want to know more about both the past and present work experiences of the audience. Are people new to the company or have they been employed for years?

Why will people attend your presentation? Is it because their attendance is required, or is it because they are really interested in the topic?

Also, how much previous knowledge on the topic of your presentation do they have? Talking over their heads can be as frustrating to people as talking down to them. You need to be aware of terminology and acronyms the audience may already be familiar with and those they may not have heard before.

Finally, you need to have an estimate of how many people will attend. This will help you in selecting the proper type of presentation media and is particularly important if you are going to provide handouts.

Characteristics

Demographic characteristics of the audience are also a major consideration. Information such as sex, age, ethnic background, and political and religious beliefs may be important in determining stories or scenarios to use for a particular audience. Avoid jokes or cartoon images that could be offensive to the audience.

If presenting within a company or organization, the corporate culture is an important consideration. Corporate culture includes conventions of dress, attitudes, morale, and the camaraderie among the workers.

Environment

When traveling to another country or even another section of the United States, people check the temperature to see what type of clothing to take. However, the presentation environment involves more than temperature and humidity.

Physical Surroundings. The physical surroundings where the presentation is to be given are extremely important. First, a map with directions can be helpful in locating both a company address and a room within a large company. If you are flying in from another city, you will need to know how far the location is from the airport and how to get from the airport to the meeting place for the presentation. Do not feel embarrassed to ask questions–it is far better to ask how long it takes to get to the meeting place than to arrive late.

A map with directions is helpful in getting to a meeting at an unfamiliar location.

Physical surroundings within the meeting room are also important. Before selecting your presentation media, you need to know whether such items as a projection screen, overhead projector, slide projector, easel, and writing board are available to use. If you arrive with a disk prepared for a computer show and find that a computer and projection system are not available, you are in trouble.

Even the type of room arrangement and the type of chairs are important in planning your strategy. For example, you may plan to have the audience meet in small groups of three or four people. Finding out upon your arrival that the chairs are all permanently fastened to the floor in an auditorium setting could put a damper on this activity.

A key element in planning is to know as much as possible in advance. However, remaining flexible is always a good motto. Last-minute adjustments must be expected and may require creative solutions only you can control.

Theme. If you are speaking at a meeting, conference, or convention, you may find that a theme has been selected. Perhaps your title and topic can incorporate the theme. In the absence of an established theme, you may want to establish your own. At any rate, your entire presentation should be planned so it compliments the general theme and any other activities of the conference.

Relationship to Other Activities. Other scheduled activities may have a bearing on your presentation. You should find out how many and what types of presentations are scheduled before, during, and after your presentation. Whether you are scheduled first in the morning, just before or after lunch, late in the afternoon, or as a luncheon or dinner speaker is important in determining your strategies.

The amount of coverage on your particular topic during a conference is another consideration. An outline or abstract of all presentations may be available for you to study in advance.

Being aware of world happenings, political activities, sports events, and local news is also important. You may want to bring up-to-date events into your talk or be aware of them in case members of the audience refer to these events. This type of information is important in conversing with individual members of the group before or during breaks.

> When presenting at a conference, select a title for your presentation to go along with the theme of the conference. You need to consider how your talk relates to other activities on the program.

Set Your Schedule

Any presentation requires preparation time. Your personal time schedule dictates what you can do. What is your presentation lead time? How much time can you devote to preparation? How much time is allowed for your presentation?

Before the Presentation

The time before a presentation consists of both long- and short-range planning. Long-range planning refers to the days, weeks, or months you have available to devote to preparation. Short-range planning involves the tasks needed upon your arrival at the presentation location.

Remember to prepare and plan ahead.

Long-Range Planning. The first consideration involves how much time is available before the presentation is to be given. A two-month lead time may be adequate—but not if your schedule is so full you cannot devote attention to your preparation. On the other hand, you may not be able to put a complete multimedia presentation together for an event that is two days away—even if you have the entire two days to work on the presentation.

Short-Range Planning. Being able to visit the room where the presentation will take place, before the time of the presentation, can help lessen your anxiety. If the chairs need to be adjusted or equipment set up, then lead time before the presentation is needed. Many conferences are so tightly scheduled that very little time is allowed for special arrangements immediately before each presentation. In this case, plan your presentation to require minimal adjustments.

In other words, be practical. Tackle only what is reasonable to accomplish in the amount of time available.

During the Presentation

Being sensitive of the allotted time for your presentation is imperative throughout your delivery because you may need to adjust. Finishing right on schedule requires planning and skill.

Speakers may feel they cannot finish their presentation because they have so many important points to share. Perhaps the real reason is they plan to accomplish too much in too little time. A speech planned for 50 minutes and delivered in 25 by simply talking fast is usually not effective. Depth of coverage of any topic should be approached differently considering the available time.

Actually, planning too much rather than too little may be a technique that gives confidence to a speaker. With a bit of clever maneuvering, last minute choices of exactly what to include can be tailored to fit the needs of the audience.

For many presentations, you will want to allow a question-and-answer session at the end. Determine the time for this activity during your planning. When audience interaction is to take place throughout the presentation, adhering to the time schedule becomes even more difficult. However, it is still essential unless no definite ending time has been established.

Some speakers like to place a watch or small clock on the podium or behind an overhead projector so they can be aware of the time. Others prefer to ask for discrete 5- or 10-minute warning signals from someone in the audience. Regardless of the technique used, remember that finishing on the scheduled time–not too early and not too late–takes careful planning and practice. It is essential for an effective presentation.

Investigate Your Resources

Good presentations are possible with a small budget, limited or no staff, and even with a very limited amount of equipment. However, these three factors, if available, may greatly enhance a presentation. A presenter must be realistic during planning about what is available during the development stage and what will be available for the presentation.

Budget

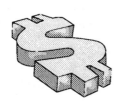

How much money can you spend on your presentation?

Determine if you have a budget and, if so, for what amount. Preparation and production of presentation media can become expensive. Labor used for preparing computer-generated overhead transparencies or slides is costly. Even handouts or bound booklets can total up to a costly amount quickly. Computer shows may be an inexpensive item if you have already developed one appropriate to use with available equipment; however, if the equipment is not provided, you may have a big rental bill to pay.

Staff

The staff time available to help you in preparing your presentation media will, no doubt, affect your planning strategy. You can prepare everything you need; but, if others are available to render assistance, call them in if the budget allows.

Equipment

Equipment available both for preparing and delivering the presentation is critical. Do not assume that whatever you want will automatically be in place at the desired time and location. Check ahead to be sure your desired presentation equipment needs will be met. Be realistic!

Establish Your Objectives

Every presenter should determine the goals or objectives for a presentation. The success of a presentation is measured by whether these established objectives are met.

Goals or objectives can also be thought of as purposes. Ask yourself, "What is my purpose?" It may be to inform, teach, sell, motivate, or persuade the audience. Actually, a presentation may include more than one purpose.

Another way of stating the purpose(s) of a presentation is to consider problems to be solved as a result of the presentation. A speech on the relocation benefits and procedures of a company planning a move to another state could be solving problems for employees as well as reducing fears for those suddenly forced to move to another location or resign.

> **Goals?**
> **Objectives?**
> **Purposes?**

Conduct Your Research

You may already be an expert on the topic for your presentation and have all the information you need. Or, you may need to research, read, and find out everything you can to become an expert. Remember that people want facts, concrete evidence, and details. You are the authority, so they expect you to be knowledgeable about the subject.

Introduction
Body
Conclusion

According to Verderber, audiences are more likely to listen and remember information that is
(1) perceived as new;
(2) emphasized;
(3) relevant; and
(4) presented creatively (Verderber, 1987).

Check Your Organization

The last step in planning your presentation strategy is to organize your material in a logical sequence. Your information should flow in a meaningful way similar to a written report. Making an outline is a good way to develop your organization. Another method is to write each of the various topics to be covered on a notecard. Then, you can rearrange the cards until you find a natural progression.

After planning the body, you need to develop an introduction and a conclusion. The introduction should be designed to set the stage and tone and gain the attention of the audience. The body provides the "meat" of your message. A conclusion may recap or summarize your main ideas. Your ending words should be chosen to make a lasting impression on the audience. Therefore, plan a strong ending.

With your strategy planned, you are ready to decide what type of media will enhance your presentation. Remember—content is most important, but media can help you present the content effectively. Chapter 3 provides you with details about various types of media available to assist you.

Reference

Verderber, Rudolph F. (1987). *The Challenge of Public Speaking.* Belmont, California: Wadsworth Publishing Company, 154-165.

Selecting Media

3

A selection process in today's world is not easy because so many choices, so many alternatives, are available. Decision making becomes a major task in today's society.

Yesterday's world consisted of far fewer options. For example, you could select vanilla, chocolate, or strawberry ice cream. Today's world offers the option of Baskin-Robbins' 31 Flavors or more, with additional choices of regular, lowfat, or nonfat ice cream. Or you could choose frozen yogurt with the same decisions of regular, lowfat, or nonfat.

Decision making can be frustrating with so many choices available. It can also be exciting because of the many unique possibilities not available in the past.

While presentation purposes are essentially the same as in the past, presentation media has been enhanced by computer technology. The production and delivery processes are more sophisticated, yet easier for the presenter.

The choices of presentation media are categorized as models, handouts, posters and flip charts, electronic copyboards, overhead transparencies, 35 mm slides, and computer-based shows. Frequently, the choice should not simply be which one to select but which ones to select. Combining media types makes a presentation both more forceful and more interesting.

Many types of presentation media are available— models, handouts, posters and flip charts, notetakers/copyboards, overhead transparencies, 35 mm slides, and computer-based shows. This chapter will explore each of these various choices to help you select one or a combination of the vast assortment of presentation media that have all been enhanced by computer technology.

Selecting and making presentation media is only part of the task. When and how to use the media appropriately also requires careful thought and study. The focus of the presentation should be on the presenter–not the media. Media is a support or an aid (remember the terminology of audiovisual aids) to a presentation. Without the right use, the intended impact of a presentation can fall short of its mark.

Models or Replicas

Models or replicas are excellent for demonstration purposes. If you are trying to motivate workers about moving to a new location several hundred miles away, you may want to give them an idea of how the new facility, presently under construction, will look when it is completed. A realistic miniature model of the facility and its community would be far more appealing than an engineering blueprint of the new facility and surrounding area.

> Enlarged models help your audience visualize small objects. Miniature models are effective if you cannot bring in the real thing.

Models can be a product shown in actual size, such as a speaker demonstrating to a small group an ergonomically designed chair using an actual chair. *Miniatures or reduced sizes* would be more appropriate if the chair was a part of the facility scenario mentioned before. If the chair controls were being demonstrated to a large group, an *enlarged* chair would allow the audience to view the demonstration better. A less expensive *replication* of the chair could serve effectively as a demonstration tool.

Advantages

Models are very realistic in either full-size or scaled versions. In the case of viewing the planned company facilities and the surrounding area, the audience has the advantage of almost being there–even though they are not physically at the facility. Thus, a model can prepare a person for the actual event. An existing model may be more convenient to acquire than making actual visuals requiring overhead or computer projection.

Limitations

Making a realistic model can be expensive. A model must be the proper size to be visible to the entire audience. And, a model may not be available.

Properly developed handouts are an effective presentation medium to use in conjunction with other types of media.

Handouts

The presentation medium used most frequently is a handout–the printed materials used during a presentation. A handout can be used by itself or with any of the other presentation media. For example, the facility model presentation would be more persuasive if accompanied by a handout including word descriptions, blueprints or layouts, maps, and photographs. Handouts are valuable to provide information during the presentation or as a resource for participants later.

Advantages

The advantages of handouts are numerous. A need for extensive notetaking by the audience is eliminated.

People not able to attend can get the handouts and catch up on what they missed.

In the development stage, artwork or photography may be adapted to the printed page. The content can be resequenced easily by the presenter. Revisions or updates of the materials are easy to make using a word processing or desktop publishing program. The materials can be produced economically, distributed easily, updated or revised periodically, and used to display still visuals.

Limitations

An audience looking at handouts during a presentation may become too involved with the printed materials and may not focus on what the speaker is saying. The sound of pages turning may be distracting both to the speaker and the audience. The audience may decide that attendance during the presentation is unnecessary, then take a handout and leave.

Preparation

Written words and the way they are presented on paper give the audience an impression of a speaker similar to the impression spoken words make. Therefore, the preparation and presentation of handouts is important. For example, if the pages are unattractively arranged and presented, the reader forms a negative impression similar to the impression formed by watching a speaker who may be untidy or "sloppy" in appearance.

Desktop-Publishing Software. Material today can look like published material instead of typewritten

> Word processing or desktop publishing software such as the ones listed below can make your handouts have a professional look.
> Microsoft Word
> PageMaker
> QuarkXPress
> Ventura Publisher
> WordPerfect

material. The page-layout capabilities of desktop-publishing software have glamorized the written page. Although desktop-publishing software has many sophisticated features over word-processing software, the distinction between them has merged. The final printed output may show very little difference.

In both cases, a page may contain type in different fonts, sizes, and styles. Lines, boxes, and shading may be included. Also, clip art, photographs, charts, and graphs may be imported from other programs. Design ideas that can make handouts attractive and more readable are important.

Design Ideas. The first design idea to consider is the effective use of space. Pages should not be cluttered. Fifty percent of the page should contain blank, or "white," space which is spread out over the page. Centered, side, and sub-headings break the monotony of text reading and serve as "road signs" in directing and focusing the reader's attention. Font sizes and styles can be varied when a distinction is needed. Fonts are available in a wide variety of typefaces; however, be careful that a different font serves a purpose, such as to emphasize or differentiate. A page with too many different font changes will be distracting.

Illustrations such as charts, graphs, or pictures create visual interest and may serve to tell the story better than written words. Cartoon figures can help to illustrate points. (More adults than children read newspaper cartoons.)

One effective way of providing a handout is to make miniatures of selected visuals from the presentation. Most desktop presentation software provides a feature allowing two, three, four, or six

Miniatures of the key visuals can be created using desktop presentation software.

miniatures to be placed on the page. Titles and footnotes can be added to the sheet if desired. The placing of three visuals vertically on the left of a page allows the listener to make notes in the column on the right.

Reproducing all of the visuals from a presentation may be an overkill; however, it is effective to include carefully selected visuals the audience may want to refer to later. Then the audience will not try to recreate the visuals in their notes.

Production

The production of handouts is also important. Considerations are the paper, the reproduction method, and the type of binding.

Paper. Handouts are probably best duplicated on normal 8 1/2- x 11-inch paper, although other sizes may be used if a purpose is served. Although the visuals used for projection may be in full color, it is probably not economical to have the handouts in full color. However, using a variety of paper colors can be effective as a coding device. For instance, a speaker can refer to the yellow sheet or the blue sheet.

Paper is available in many new colors and textures. The paper you select can make your handouts unique–and can help to set any tone from flamboyant to conservative to distinguished.

Reproduction Methods. Handouts may be reproduced using a copier or other printing process. Good quality reproduction is needed for readability purposes as well as for creating a positive impression on an audience.

Binding. Handouts may be several loose sheets, or they may be arranged in a particular sequence and bound as a package. They may be stapled together or inserted into a notebook of some type. A notebook increases the cost but is effective in organizing several materials and providing a personalized "take-home" booklet that serves as a reference.

Distribution

When you provide handouts for the audience, be sure to prepare enough for everyone. If a larger than expected audience shows up for a conference presentation, you can get a list of names and addresses and mail handouts to those not receiving them. With the high cost of postage and the extra effort of addressing and mailing involved, it is usually easier to prepare more handouts than needed rather than run the risk of not having enough. An audience will generally want the handouts immediately–not next week.

Appropriateness. A speaker should consider the appropriateness of materials and when they should be distributed. Members of an audience may feel they have gained more if they can take away tangible evidence–such as handouts or a booklet–for future use or reference. On the other hand, only material that will be useful to the majority of the audience should be distributed. If materials are found in a trash can outside the door, you have a strong hint, for the next time around, that the handouts probably did not really serve a purpose.

If members of the audience show an interest in an item not available during the presentation, you may want to follow up by getting a list of names and addresses or by collecting business cards from those

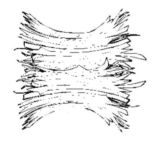

Too many handouts can become costly to you and a burden to your audience.

wanting the additional information. Caution should be taken, however, to promise only what you will deliver.

When. Authorities disagree on when to distribute handouts. Some say handouts are distracting and take the audience's attention away from the speaker. Therefore, they prefer to wait and distribute them after the presentation.

If audience members are to refer to the handouts, they will need them at the beginning of the presentation. Then they can see what is in them and know whether they need to take notes. However, to keep control of an audience's attention, you need to tell them specifically what they should be looking at in the handouts and when they should be listening to you.

Handouts can be distributed before the presentation begins by placing them on the desks or chairs before people enter the room. A helper can distribute handouts to the audience as they come into the room or at some other point during the presentation.

If a helper is not available to distribute handouts, an audience member can be drafted. A speaker distributing handouts from the front of the room can give the stack to a person on the side of the first row and ask that person to count out the number needed for the row, then pass the rest of the stack to the next row. Usually, the end persons all catch on and will do the same. This technique speeds up the distribution considerably compared to the whole stack being passed to each person. You may want to hold remarks until all materials are distributed.

In any event, distributing a collated package of handouts is less confusing than distributing numerous

Determine the best time to distribute your handouts.

Before
During
After

handouts one by one throughout the meeting. However, this rule can be violated with a reason. For instance, a particular sheet may be kept until a certain point of the presentation to maintain an element of surprise.

If handouts are used for resource materials only, place them on a table at the back of the room for participants to pick up as they exit. This is convenient for the participants because of traffic flow; however, a similar stack could be placed at the front of the room for those individuals who wish to come forward to talk with you.

Posters and Flip Charts

Posters and flip charts can be made in a wide variety of sizes. Posters can be displayed throughout the presentation as they are usually made on a stiff paperboard. You can have a stack of posters and reveal them one by one or display them around the room so all posters are in view at all times. Flip charts usually consist of thinner paper attached to a pad and placed on an easel board.

Posters are frequently thought of as a presentation media more appropriate for elementary schools, and flip charts as a device used in training sessions. These stereotyped uses are not the only uses. Similar to other presentation media, both posters and flip charts have distinct advantages as well as limitations.

Advantages

Posters or flip charts can be made before the presentation and carried into the presentation for use.

No special equipment is needed—other than a place to show the materials. Flip charts also can be developed during the presentation. By using marking pens, the presenter or a member of the audience can use the flip charts for recording key points. This procedure is effective during brainstorming sessions.

As a flip chart is completed, it can be torn from the pad and attached to the wall with masking tape (assuming this is allowed in the meeting facility). Thus, a chronological record of the presentation is shown on the wall to aid discussion. Late arrivals have a quick view of what has occurred before their arrival.

Limitations

Posters and flip charts are appropriate for audiences with a dozen or so participants. If care is taken to make the writing large, they may work successfully for an audience of 15 or 20. Similar to using a chalkboard, the presenter's back must be to the audience while writing on the flip chart. However, a pre-made poster or flip chart allows the presenter to use a pointer and face the audience. Writing or printing must be large to be legible from a distance.

Preparation

To determine if print is large enough, try reading the poster or flip chart from a distance equal to the farthest distance viewers will be seated. Since many people write on a board unevenly, light-blue lines can serve as a guide and will not be seen by the audience. You can purchase poster paper with light-blue grid lines, or you could lightly draw the lines before the presentation.

In some instances, you may find the traditional chalkboard a useful tool. Whiteboards using colored marking pens are also available.

Three or four colored markers can help highlight points as well as add variety. To avoid "see-through writing," some presenters use only every other page in a flip chart pad when they are developing flip charts in advance. The pages can be taped or stapled together for easy turning.

Too much writing on a poster or flip chart can reduce its impact. The design principles given in Chapter 6–"Designing the Visuals"–apply to both posters and flip charts as well as overhead transparencies and slides.

The preparation of posters or flip charts has traditionally been a manual method. However, computers and other equipment can now be used to prepare more appealing products.

Courtesy of Quartet Manufacturing Company.

Manual. The traditional way of preparing posters or flip charts is by using marking pens in a variety of colors. Illustrations or pictures also can be pasted on the posters or flip charts.

Electronic. Text layout can be prepared using computers to take advantage of typography capabilities for a variety of fonts, sizes, and styles. Computer programs such as TypeStyler can provide special effects such as stretching the type into interesting shapes. Illustrations can be added with draw programs or by importing clip art or scanned photographs. After a master copy is printed on standard 8 1/2- x 11-inch paper, special equipment–such as a ChartPrinter–can produce easel-pad-size flip charts.

Courtesy of Minnesota Western Visual Presentation Systems.

Notetakers/Copyboards

Notetakers/copyboards are available to aid in meetings for recording the notes and interaction of the group by writing on a board and then making copies of the board for members of the audience. The board looks like a regular write-on board, but a device is attached to produce a paper copy of the words and illustrations written, drawn, or even taped to the board surface. Copies are produced from the board by scanning the image to make a copy. Several companies manufacture these products, and they vary in how they operate and in the quality of output.

Courtesy of Quartet
Manufacturing Company.

Overhead Transparencies

Overhead transparencies are also called view graphs or foils. An overhead projector needed to project the transparencies is relatively inexpensive and commonly found in both meeting rooms and classrooms.

The use of overhead transparencies has many advantages and a few limitations for users. These advantages and limitations are discussed next.

Advantages

Unlike writing on a flip chart or a board, the speaker or presenter can face the audience throughout the presentation. Since a speaker needs to maintain eye contact with the audience as much as possible, maintaining eye contact while showing a visual is helpful. The audience does not feel left out, and discussion and participation are easier.

Overhead transparencies can be made spontaneously by writing on acetate film with special markers in a variety of colors. Materials also can be prepared before the presentation by hand or, more professionally, by computer. Word-processing or

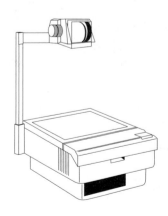

desktop-publishing programs can be used to make transparencies; however, presentation software offers many benefits.

A distinct advantage of overhead transparencies over 35 mm slides is that changes (deletions or adjustments to the sequencing order) can be made minutes before the presentation or even during the presentation itself. For instance, if your presentation is taking longer than anticipated, you may need to avoid showing a few of the visuals in order to keep on a time schedule. Also, overhead transparencies can be viewed in fully-lighted rooms.

Limitations

Overhead transparencies may not be appropriate for large rooms and auditoriums. Experiment to see if the projected visual can be easily read from any seat in the room; however, you may not always be able to do this in advance. The print of typewritten visuals is far too small for distance viewing and will strain the audience. Visuals simply typewritten with no enlargement should not be used. Transparencies look much better in frames, but these take up considerably more room than slides in a briefcase or suitcase.

Placing the visuals on the projector and removing them can become distracting as well as time consuming. You must stand right by the projector to change the visuals. If you are on a platform using a microphone, a helper can sit near the overhead projector and change the visuals at the appropriate times. This process should be rehearsed so the helper develops the proper timing sequence of changing the visuals. If you have to nod or ask for the visual to be changed repeatedly, thought patterns can be broken—for both the speaker and the audience.

Preparation

Preparing overhead transparencies involves gathering the right type of products for use as well as following good design techniques. Chapter 6 covers design techniques appropriate for all types of media; however, a few special design techniques for transparencies are mentioned in this section.

Write-On Method. Overhead projection marker pens (available in a variety of colors with fine or broad tips) are available for use in preparing transparencies. The hand-made look can be an effective delivery method because it is spontaneous. Preparation can be accomplished minutes before the presentation when a computer and a printer are unavailable. The effect of using such visuals can be that of "I made these a few minutes ago especially for you" versus "my secretary made this canned presentation several speeches back."

Color. In addition to using colored markers, a presenter can bring the audience out of the monochrome world by using colored transparencies. A rainbow package, for instance, includes blue, pink, yellow, and green overheads. This tinted background can be more stimulating than using clear transparencies and can reduce glare.

Transparencies are also available that, when reproduced by a thermofax (heat process), will develop with a colored image on clear acetate—such as red, blue, or green on clear. Another type produces yellow images on a dark blue, red, or green background.

Color highlight film is a special write-on film coated with a vivid blue emulsion. When you use

Courtesy of Minnesota Western Visual Presentation Systems.

Transparencies
- ✔ Advantages
- ✔ Limitations
- ✔ **Preparation**
- ✔ Production

special color highlight pens (red, green, or orange), the emulsion disappears and color from the marker remains making a dramatic, sparkling image right before the audience's eyes. An overlay of this color film sheet can be placed over a prepared visual and the highlight marker used to circle, underline, or highlight important points. A special eraser allows you to erase the markings for use in your next presentation.

Full-color images can be produced with ink-jet, thermal-transfer, or laser printers. Color technology has made full-color visuals for overhead transparencies a reality. With the necessary equipment, the beautiful, vivid color of slides can be printed on overhead transparencies.

Production

Even though it is possible to produce overhead transparencies through photographic methods (similar to 35 millimeter slides), overhead transparencies are normally produced by thermofax, photocopiers, or laser printers.

Thermofax. The thermofax is a machine that serves as a popular means of developing the transparencies. An original master is placed behind the transparency and then fed into the machine. The imaged transparency and the master emerge from the machine. Since the thermofax works on a heat process, the transparency may curl–making the use of a frame mount more important.

Photocopiers. Many users today prefer to use their copying machine for making transparencies. Transparencies specially made for copiers are available in several different weights or thicknesses. (Transparencies made for the thermofax are not of the right weight and may melt on the copier drum causing serious damage.) When transparency sheets are fed through the copier instead of paper, toner adheres to each sheet.

Laser Printers. Overhead transparencies also can be made by placing transparency sheets in the paper tray of a laser printer. As with a copier, be careful to use the right type of transparency. They are heavier than thermofax transparencies. Special overheads for laser printers can be purchased, although overheads for copiers can be used. Caution should be followed, however, as transparency film that is not heavy enough can melt and ruin the printer drum.

Color Printers. Technology uses several other different techniques to print in full color. Laser printers use colored toners. Ink-jet printers apply the colors in a spraying process while thermal transfer printers use layers of color film to transfer the color to paper or an overhead transparency.

You can make either clear or tinted color background transparencies by using film with a thermofax, a photo-copier, or a laser printer.

35 Millimeter Slides

A sophisticated type of presentation media is 35 mm slides. Although the preparation of the original is similar, the techniques of production are different. Colors are very sharp and clear, and slides are associated as a tool for the very professional presenter. The technology of today makes the production easier and faster than in the past.

Advantages

Slides are small, convenient to use, and relatively inexpensive. You could add slides or rearrange them as needed while preparing the presentation.

Actual camera shots may be included in addition to computer-generated visuals. Since you can change slides with a handheld (possibly cordless) remote control, a large number of slides can be viewed quickly and smoothly in contrast with having to change transparencies on an overhead projector.

Limitations

For slides, the room needs to be darkened for effective viewing. Thus, the audience may not be able to see you and vice versa. As a result, interaction with the audience may be reduced or completely eliminated.

Film must be shot and processed, which requires you to allow sufficient preparation time. One-hour developing is available in metropolitan areas. Since slides are arranged in a tray, you cannot rearrange or eliminate a few slides to meet audience needs or time restraints during your presentation.

In using a slide projector, you need to darken the room for effective viewing.

Production

You can produce 35 mm slides in several ways. The first method has been available for years and involves the traditional focus-and-shoot technique. The second method is a more recent technology development and involves the use of a film recorder. In either case, the exposed film must be processed.

Computer to Camera. Shooting directly from the computer to a camera involves taking a picture of the computer display. Slides produced in this matter may show a loss in quality when compared to the original.

Computer to Film Recorder. A film recorder is a peripheral device that allows computer images to become 35 mm slides. It contains a lightproof box with a back (photographic jargon for camera) aimed at a tiny cathode-ray tube which displays the image to be recorded on film.

The camera back on a film recorder is normally a 35 mm camera, but it can be substituted by an insta-matic camera to create 4- x 5-inch transparencies. The original purpose of these small transparencies was to shoot a test slide; however, enlargers are available that allow users to project these miniature overheads on the screen. In addition, overhead projectors are available that enlarge the projected image for the audience. Much less space is required to store these miniatures.

Courtesy of Presentation Technologies.

The process of creating slides is as easy as telling the computer to print a laser copy. A slide is created by opening the image file from within the film recorder software and giving the print command. Depending upon the particular film recorder and the resolution desired, the imaging of each slide may take between two and ten minutes. Therefore, the shooting of a roll of film (24 or 36 slides) can require between six and eight hours. Since this process ties up the computer, many companies will batch the slides to the film recorder for shooting during the night hours.

Hardcopy to Slidemaker. A slidemaker enables you to make slides directly from your hard copy. This device is convenient if you have a photo or other camera-ready material and have no need to generate the material for the slide from your computer.

Computer-Based Media

A computer-based show eliminates the need for overhead transparencies and 35 mm slides because computer-generated slides are displayed directly on a computer screen or projected for viewing by larger groups. The projection methods for this newly developing area of computer-based shows are classified as LCD (liquid crystal display) panels, projection units, videoshow devices, or videotape.

Courtesy of nView Corporation.

LCD panels or pads are flat-panel units connected to a computer and placed on an overhead projector. The devices allow you to project information displayed on the computer screen. Most units presently in use are monochrome, although more expensive units are available that will project in color. A mouse-controlled pointer on the computer screen will project to focus audience attention on a specific point on the screen.

Projection units represent a direct computer-to-projector system of creating an on-screen presentation. Units can be permanently mounted on the ceiling or a high wall. As with the projection panel, a mouse-controlled pointer is useful in highlighting or emphasizing various points on the screen. Such units fall into a higher price range; however, clear and colorful projections are possible.

Other types of video presentation devices are coming to the forefront in the rapidly-developing technical world. For instance, you can create a presentation on a computer in your office and then go to the presentation and use a videoshow device. This device uses random-access technology to retrieve images from your disk.

Another alternative is to convert the computer images to videotape by use of a special card in the computer and a connected videorecorder. Announcements or voice-overs can be edited into the final production.

Advantages

The advantages of computer-based shows are many. Very professional shows in full color are possible. Many of the specialized software programs have a screen or slide-show option that allows you to program how the images will advance. The user might key in the number of seconds between visuals, advance to the next image by clicking any key on the computer, or go to a specific slide by simply keying in its number. Information can be modified spontaneously to reflect new information or audience input.

Many presentation programs include dramatic special effects or transition possibilities that are used when the screens change to the next image. These special effects can be fades, wipes, or dissolves similar to those used in a television studio.

> A computer-based show can be transferred to videotape by using a special card in the computer and a connected videorecorder.

Limitations

The main limitation of a computer-based show is high cost—or stated in another way, the expense of hardware/software/peripherals. Because this technology is advancing so rapidly, equipment will become obsolete rapidly. The equipment may not be available in the right place at the right time. For instance, visuals carried to a meeting on a disk are useless if compatible equipment is not available to project the contents of the disk. Presenters also may find their presentations are relatively inflexible.

Preparation and Production

Preparation for a computer show is very similar—using the same software—to making computer-generated visuals for overhead transparencies or slides. However, additional software can be used to create multimedia productions, as described in Chapter 12.

> ### Service Bureaus
>
> A service bureau provides several alternatives for presentation-software users. Rather than purchasing a film recorder, you may prefer to send data files by disk or modem to a service bureau for shooting and processing. Service bureaus have sprung up throughout the country to produce presentation-graphics materials as well as desktop-published items.
>
> You may prefer to purchase your own equipment and train personnel to operate it. A payback period for the necessary equipment can be calculated based on the projected number of visuals to be produced on a monthly or yearly basis. However, if the output equipment is not available, you may find it feasible to use your own data disks but rely on a service bureau to record and develop the film. Some service bureaus will take written text and turn it into visuals. Of course, this labor intensive task is quite expensive.

You can send your slides either on disk or through a modem to service bureaus such as Genigraphics for development.

In developing your visuals, you should keep in mind that the size dimensions are different for the various types of media. Even though with desktop presentation packages you may select the size by

checking an appropriate box, you need to be aware of
the ratios (vertical by horizontal) listed below:

Poster	Unlimited
Overhead Transparencies	4 x 5*
35 mm Slides	2 x 3
Video	3 x 4

*Frame openings are 7 1/2 x 9 1/2, 7 1/2 x 10, or 8 x
10 inches. Be sure you check the size of the frames you
are going to use before making your transparencies.

Developing the Message

A graphic director for *Time* magazine states, "The information put into the pages of the magazine is not the most important factor—what really counts is what remains in the minds of the readers." Thus, to develop an effective presentation, you must carefully plan and develop the presentation message. Your goal as a presenter is to deliver a message that accomplishes its purpose—to inform, teach, motivate, sell, or persuade—not to impress the audience with how great you are as a speaker and how much you know.

A content outline is a logical first step in formulating the message for a presentation. Once you are satisfied with the topics and their sequence, a storyboard is a good vehicle to use to develop visuals.

A storyboard is a visual outline of a presentation that helps the presenter develop visual images to correlate with the verbal message. A writer uses an outline; an engineer uses a blueprint; a systems programmer uses a flowchart. A presenter's parallel tool is the storyboard.

In developing a storyboard, a good method is to use a sheet of paper or a notecard for each main point or fact from the content outline. Ideas, thoughts, and images can be sketched onto each page/notecard. Do not worry if these pages are messy and cluttered at this point.

A content outline is needed to develop the presentation message. A storyboard will help determine how the message is best shared. A message can be expressed in many different ways by using words, numbers, diagrams, artwork, or photographs. Before designing visuals, decisions must be made on the way information is to be illustrated. Restraint is needed in displaying the presentation message.

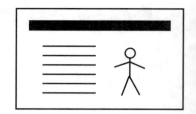

Actual words and pictures should be placed in appropriate positions—if you cannot draw, just make a circle and describe the picture in word form. Place quotations or annotations on the same page or on an attached notes page.

Some people prefer to sketch the storyboard in miniature by placing four to six visuals on a single page. However, using a single page or notecard allows pages or cards to be rearranged to try out the points in various sequences if an outline needs adjusting. Also, single pages and cards can be inserted or deleted easily as certain points need more development and other points are streamlined.

You may prefer to do this drafting and sketching by hand (with a pencil, so you can change your mind easily). Or, you may prefer to use a word-processing or outline program on your computer for creating a draft.

Before you can perfect the storyboard, you need to follow guidelines given in this chapter for developing the message as well as design principles given in Chapter 6.

Sharing Information

A presenter has many options to use in sharing information on visuals—words, numbers, diagrams, artwork, and photographs. Variety is helpful in maintaining audience interest; however, simplicity and consistency are important, also. Each visual should reinforce the spoken words.

Words

Text charts can display words in several ways. Choices include: titles, bullet lists, build series, column charts, and paragraphs.

Titles. An opening visual is similar to a title page for a report. A title visual should include the topic of the presentation, identification of the presenter–name, title, position, and company–and optional information, such as date, company logo, etc. Since presenters frequently like to display the title visual as people are entering the presentation room, you may want to include a theme design to set the tone of the presentation.

Bullet Lists. Bullet lists help the viewers follow point by point as you speak. A bullet list may use a bullet or other symbols such as boxes, arrows, hands, stars, etc., to begin each item in the list.

Build Series. Rather than displaying a bullet list all at once, you may use a build series containing several visuals. The first visual contains only one bulleted item, then a separate visual is used to add another point. This is very effective, because each point is displayed precisely when you are ready for it–the audience cannot read ahead.

Another way to use a build series is to show all six points on six slides. You can highlight the point being discussed in a bright color and de-emphasize the other points by using a dim color.

Some presentation programs prepare build series automatically. If yours does not, a build series is easy to make. Prepare and save the final visual with all points, then save additional separate visuals as you remove one point at a time.

Column Charts. Charts with two or three columns can be used to show simple lists. You can draw lines and divide the visual into one, two, or three parts. Be careful, because too much information on the chart will make it difficult to read.

The Message

The message can be displayed as
- Words

The Message

The message can be displayed as
- Words
- Numbers

The Message

The message can be displayed as
- Words
- Numbers
- Diagrams

The Message

The message can be displayed as
- Words
- Numbers
- Diagrams
- Artwork / Illustrations / Photographs

Bullet lists arrange items in a vertical list. A build series highlights each item on separate visuals. This technique is particularly helpful when you are creating 35 mm slides or computer-based screen shows.

Paragraphs. Quotations or a short sentence can be used on a visual to emphasize a particular point. However, be careful of filling a chart with too many words–a rule of thumb is 49 words (seven words on seven lines) or less on a visual.

Numbers

Simply reproducing spreadsheet output does not produce an appropriate visual for comprehending numbers. The output would look cluttered, and the print would be too small to read. However, with a spreadsheet program and its graphics capabilities, you can make visuals as charts and graphs to effectively show numerical relationships. Presentation graphics programs provide even more flexibility and sophistication.

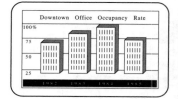

When precise data must be displayed, a table is still appropriate (but use sparingly). Readability and visual appeal can be improved with large print and graphic enhancements.

Details for designing charts representing numerical information will be discussed in Chapter 5.

Diagrams

Lines, boxes, or arrows are helpful in making flow-charts, organizational charts, or other types of diagrams to show sequencing or natural order and flow. Lines and shapes help people grasp concepts better than using only word lists.

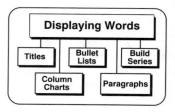

Artwork/Illustrations/Photographs

A picture is worth a thousand words–or more. If you are directing people to your home, they normally would prefer a map over a word description. Artwork and illustrations can be created from scratch using computer and drawing programs; imported as clip art from commercial or public domain programs; or made by using a scanner to digitize drawings or pictures from other sources.

Establishing the Focus

The focus of a presentation can be established by the title and subtitle. Then, it can be incorporated throughout the presentation. A master or template is useful for items that will appear in all the visuals, such as the main title, the subtitle, company logo, line art, or graphics. Even a color scheme can be designed on the master visual.

Using a master or template for this information not only speeds up production but also creates a theme of continuity for the visuals. With the general layout and selected information on each visual, the task of creating the variable information becomes much easier. Only the main idea or message needs to be added to each visual.

Exercising Creative Restraint

Use restraint in creating your message. Be concise, follow parallel structure, and, in general, avoid punctuation and abbreviations.

Be Concise

- --------------------
- --------------------
- --------------------

Concise Content

Forget the expression "If a little is good, a lot must be much better." Restrain yourself from giving your whole report, page by page, on the visuals. Instead, pick key words or expressions to represent your ideas.

Learning to express yourself in a concise manner is a real skill that may go against your past experience. During school years, you may have been asked to write 10-page papers or 2,500-word essays. In business, your reports may be lengthy and detailed. Now, you are being asked to express yourself in as few words as possible. This adjustment may be difficult to make.

The key words you select will serve as reminders to you and reinforcers for your audience. Length can confuse or muddle rather than assist in getting a point across and having it remembered.

Parallel Structure

Parallel structure refers to the sequencing of words within the sentences or phrases used in lists. If you begin a word list with verbs, follow through and begin each item in the list with a verb. If you use nouns or gerunds (verbs with "-ing" endings), do the same in each case. Consistent, parallel structure on titles and word lists is essential.

Punctuation

Often, punctuation is unnecessary on visuals. Periods are small and hard to see. Since full phrases rather than full sentences are preferred for word lists, you really do not need the period anyway.

Developing the Message

- Sharing Information
- Establishing the Focus
- Exercising Creative Restraint
- Setting the Tone

or

Develop the Message

- Share Information
- Establish the Focus
- Exercise Creative Restraint
- Set the Tone

Be concise and parallel. Use develop, share, establish, exercise, or set or developing, sharing, establishing, exercising, and setting.

Special characters, such as those available in a font called Zapf Dingbats, can make extremely large punctuation marks whenever you feel you really need to have punctuation marks. For instance, you may want to show a quotation; extra large quotations marks are better because they will be clear and readable.

Abbreviations/Acronyms

Does everyone in your audience understand your abbreviations or acronyms?

NBEA AVA ABC
CBEA CVA IFMA

Avoid abbreviations. They confuse the issue even though they may shorten a line. If you have acronyms you are certain are known by everyone in the audience, you may use them. Be concise, but not at the risk of confusing your audience.

Setting the Tone

The tone of your visuals sets the tone for your presentation. If your audience is conservative, you may want to follow along and make your visuals conservative. For instance, subdued colors might be appropriate for a meeting of doctors on the subject of cancer. For a motivational meeting of sales representatives, a flamboyant tone could be conveyed with a vivid background and lots of clip art. With a more casual group, you may want to use cartoons or casual expressions in your presentation. A board meeting may require a more conservative and dignified tone.

When you have a serious message, you will want to restrict the tone conveyed by the visuals. Keep in mind, however, that even serious people appreciate a sense of humor and need to laugh now and then.

In general, consider very carefully the effect your visuals may have to be sure you are creating the type of message you want to share with the audience. Diagrams and graphs are effective ways of illustrating information and concepts. The next chapter will provide you with ideas of how diagrams and graphs can be creatively used in designing your presentation.

Using Diagrams and Graphs

5

Graphics, according to the dictionary, refers to pictorial information. However, a graph is defined as a diagram representing the relationship between two varying sizes by means of a curve or series of lines. For clarity, this chapter will refer to the software used to create many forms of graphs and diagrams as graphics programs; the actual graphs created will be called either graphs or charts.

Traditionally, business communication has consisted of written words and numbers. Since graphs were so hard to construct by hand, reports usually were prepared with only written paragraphs and tables. Today's computer graphics software makes it possible to construct a wide variety of graphs directly from a computer spreadsheet or from simple data entry. These easy-to-prepare graphs illustrate relationships and trends much better than text and tables.

The meaning of statistical information is easier to understand when portrayed visually. In her article, "Data and Vision," Kathleen K. Wiegner says,

> The mind can see better than it can count. And so computer graphics may help people see what is not visible in a column of numbers or a stack of ledger pages. . . . The human vision system is in itself a powerful computer, taking up about 50 percent of the brain. Why not enlist this

The emphasis of this chapter is on how diagrams and graphs can be used to illustrate various types of information and concepts visually. For instance, when describing an acre as 43,560 square feet or 4,047 square meters, the concept could be illustrated by showing a drawing of a football field with the end zones marked out. With this visual, most people would be able to conceptualize an image of the size of an acre.

visual system to help solve intellectual problems? (*Forbes*, October 15, 1990)

The brain is divided into two parts functioning like central processing units. The left side processes and analyzes logical information, data, and concepts. The right side concerns itself with spatial and artistic information and ideas. Right brain knowledge is achieved through images, not words.

Of course, the two halves are present in all people, but one side of the brain is usually dominant. People with a dominating right brain hemisphere are more artistic people; they analyze complex interrelationships more effectively if information is presented graphically. Since logical people, who are left brain hemisphere dominant, are likely to grasp information either way, graphics is a tool for reaching everyone more effectively.

> Right brain dominant people are more artistic and achieve through images, not words. Logical people, who are left brain hemisphere dominant, grasp information either way. Therefore, graphics is a tool for reaching everyone more effectively.

Kinds of Diagrams and Graphs

In many books about computer graphics, the terms charts and graphs are used interchangeably. Simple text charts for making either titles or bullet lists were discussed in Chapter 4. However, this chapter deals with more complex kinds of charts or graphs than those discussed before.

The first category is referred to as diagrams (for lack of a more descriptive term) and may include data in either word or numeric format or a combination of both. Graphs dealing specifically with numeric data will be discussed in the next section.

Diagrams

The category of diagrams is very broad, but includes images showing either spatial or place relationships or process paths. Examples of each of these diagrams are described next.

Place. Place types of diagrams include organizational charts, maps, and scale drawings. Examples of typical uses are:

✔ *Organizational charts* show the relative positions, roles, and responsibilities of individuals as well as departments within a company.

✔ *Maps* show travel routes, display information by territory, or demonstrate approximate locations and sizes–whether within a company facility, the state, the country, or the world.

✔ *Scale drawings* or floor plans show layouts of arrangements drawn to scale so people can get an idea of both size and placement of a new office or an entire facility.

Process. Process diagrams fall into the general categories of flowcharts and time lines.

✔ *Flowcharts* are useful in showing the steps involved in completing an activity or work task.

✔ *Time lines* show how long various steps will take in completing the project. Various types of time lines include PERT charts (Program Evaluation Review Technique), Gantt Charts, and Critical Path Method (CPM).

Place Diagrams

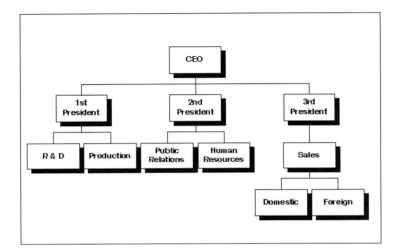

An organizational chart is useful for showing staff positions.

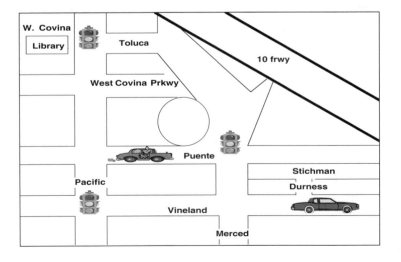

Maps are useful in directing people to a specific location.

Place Diagrams

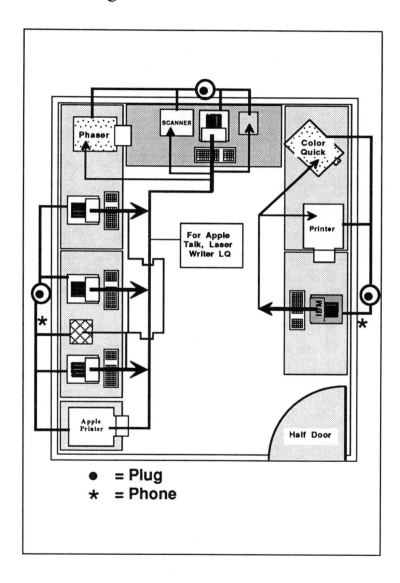

Floor plans drawn to scale are helpful in planning the layout for a new facility.

Process Diagrams

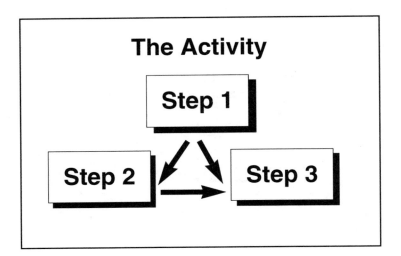

Flowcharts are useful in showing the steps involved and the progression through which these steps should move. This diagram represents a situation where you might progress to Step 3 directly or by first going through Step 2.

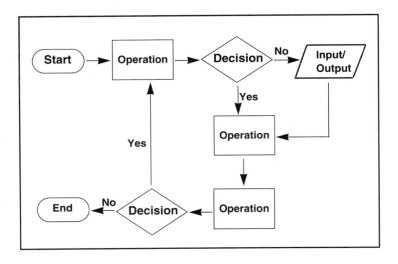

Flowcharts are also good for typical workflow involving operations and decisions.

Process Diagrams

A Gantt Chart is helpful in illustrating the time various activities will take for a work project to be completed.

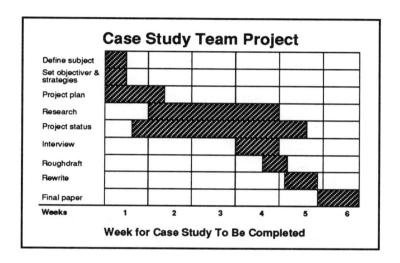

A Pert Chart is useful in illustrating the critical paths of how a work project can be most efficiently completed.

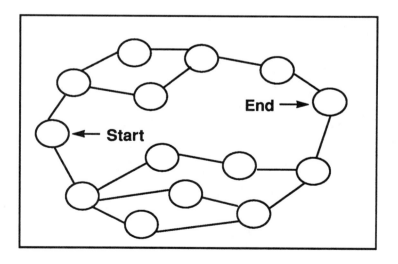

Numeric Graphs

People often use a spreadsheet to input data into a computer to construct a graph showing relationships, comparisons, and changes. Data can be directly linked to presentation programs for a more sophisticated appearance. These programs provide a number of different graph types with many layout options. Graphs can convey information and concepts to audiences by showing the relative proportions of data sets.

The objectives of what you are trying to show will determine which type of graph you should use. You may want to show frequency distributions, time-related events, comparison of component parts, comparison of places or things, or correlations.

Common numeric graphs are pie, bar, and variations of line, area, and scattergram. Each type is best suited to represent particular relationships.

Pie. A pie chart is a simple and effective way to dramatize proportional relationships by dividing a whole into relative parts. Each slice of the pie indicates a relative proportion of the total amount. The pie slices must always add up to 100 percent.

If more than six divisions of the pie are made, the pie slices may be too small and difficult to interpret. Place labels to identify each slice outside but near the slices.

A pie chart.

A pie can appear 3-dimensional by adding shading or can be exploded by pulling out one or more slices. In addition, a slice can show lines extended from one side, and then have a chart showing a breakdown within that particular slice.

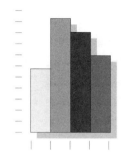

A bar chart.

Bar. Bar charts can be constructed either horizontally or vertically. Vertical bar charts also are called column charts. If possible, bar charts should be restricted to five bars or less for effective viewing.

✔ *Vertical or column bars* are effective to show quantity relationships or how something changes over time. Time series data is best displayed by showing changes in time from left to right with the height of the bars indicating the data value for each period. Data shown on the horizontal axis is called the X axis, and data shown on the vertical axis is called the Y axis.

✔ *Horizontal bar charts/graphs* are appropriate for comparing or showing relationships between sets of data. If possible, place the bars in descending order with the largest starting at the top.

✔ *Paired horizontal bars* are effective in comparing negative/positive sets of data. A zero is placed in the middle of the graph; negative numbers read from zero to the left and the positive numbers from zero to the right. This chart would be effective to compare the sales of a company's divisions that had increased to those that had decreased.

✔ Several sets of data can be displayed by using either *clustered bar charts* or *stacked bar charts.* Clustered bar charts are effective for making comparisons. Stacked bars do not effectively show comparisons but emphasize the total.

✔ *Deviation bars* to the right or left of the reference axis (a vertical centered bar) can be used to show the area of standard deviation, or the differences from an expected value. This technique can be used on either a horizontal or vertical bar graph.

Line. Line charts show trends over a series of time periods by connecting the data points. Rather than showing specific values, as in a bar graph, a general trend is shown. In contrast to the bar graph, many data points can be charted without confusing the visual. You can show a comparison of several trends by using multiple lines. The lines can be differentiated by using colors, line thicknesses, or styles–such as dots and dashes as well as a solid line.

Area. The area chart is a "filled-in" line chart. It also can show stacked chart information. The emphasis of an area chart is on the combination of the data values. This chart needs more viewing time for the combination to be grasped by the viewers. How the data sets are layered is an important sequencing decision.

Scattergram. Correlation of two data sets is shown by a scattergram. Points are plotted in reference to two independent scales in a matrix-type chart. A pattern of points can be observed with a statistically computed regression line. Since a scattergram is more technical than many of the other charts and may be more difficult to understand by audiences, it should be used with caution in presentations. Be sure of the technical level of your audience before designing your graphs.

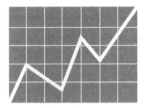

A line chart.

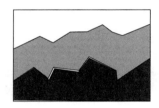

An area chart.

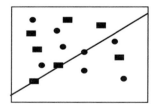

A scattergram.

Graphs

Pie charts or graphs show the proportional relationships by dividing a whole into parts. Tips in using pie graphs are:
- Use rounded numbers.
- Keep the pie slices at a minimum–four or five or less.
- Make labels short and place them next to the slices.
- Use contrasting patterns or colors.
- Restrict a visual to showing only one or two pies.

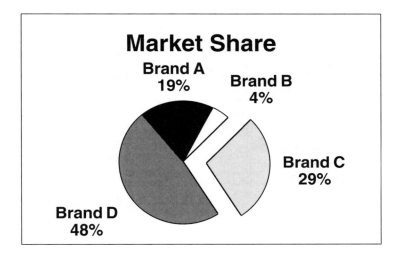

Vertical or column bars can show changes over a period of time. Tips in making bar charts or graphs are:
- Limit the number of bars to five if possible.
- Omit non-essential grid lines and tick marks.
- Make labels read horizontally rather than vertically.
- Use large bold letters for the labels.

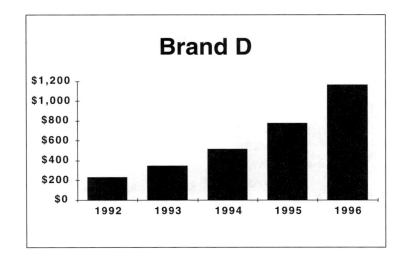

Graphs

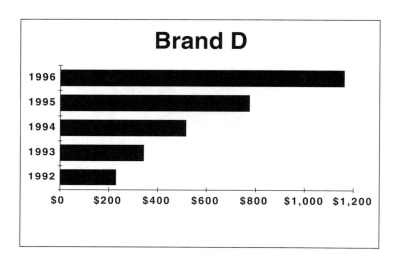

Horizontal bar charts or graphs are helpful in comparing the size or magnitude of a group of items. Tips for using bar graphs are:

- Arrange data so that bars are in either ascending or descending order.
- Use one color or fill pattern for all bars in a single data set.
- Keep X axis labels short for easier reading.

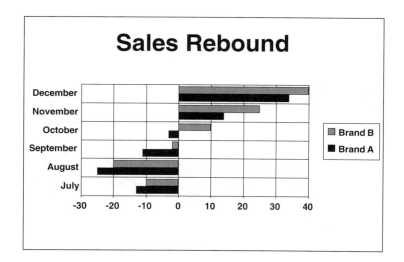

Paired horizontal bars compare negative/positive sets of data. A zero is placed in the middle of the graph with negative numbers reading to the left and positive numbers to the right.

Another variation is to use deviations bars to show the area of standard deviation or the differences from the expected value.

Graphs

Clustered bar charts or graphs are effective in making comparisons. Keep the graph simple enough to allow a quick comprehension of what the data is portraying.

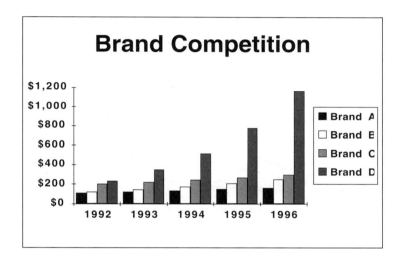

Stacked bar charts or graphs are helpful in making comparisons that emphasize the total. For a more appealing appearance, use a darker color at the bottom and make shading progressively lighter as the stacks build to the top.

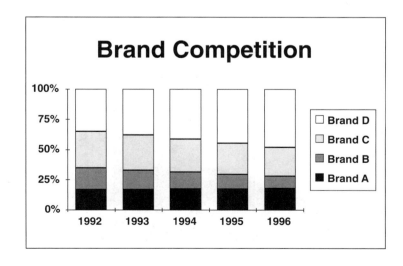

Graphs

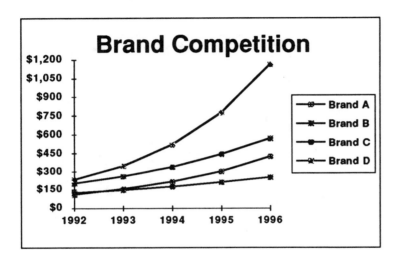

Line charts or graphs are similar to bar graphs but are more useful in showing trends over a series of time periods.

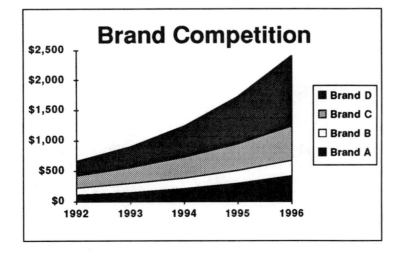

Area charts or graphs are filled-in line graphs. They are particularly useful for comparing relationships between volume or quantities. Tips in making area charts are:

- Place the biggest data at the base.
- Use the darkest color or pattern as the base.
- Keep labels horizontal.
- Allow more viewing time for an area chart to be comprehended by the audience.

Graphs

Scattergrams are useful for correlating two data sets. A statistically computed regression line is possible. A scattergram may be too technical for a visual unless you make it simple and consider the technical level of your audience.

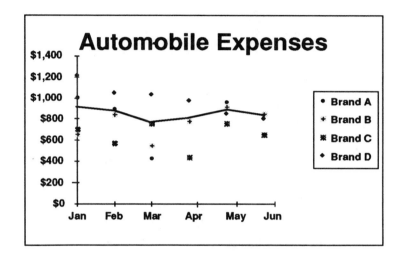

Combinations of the various types of charts or graphs are also possible. For instance, a pie can be exploded to show a breakdown of that particular segment.

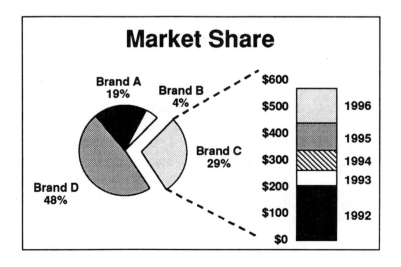

Graph Elements

Graphs have a technical language all their own. A few basic terms you should be familiar with before using presentation or graphics software are: *scale, X and Y axes, grid, tick marks, labels,* and *legend.*

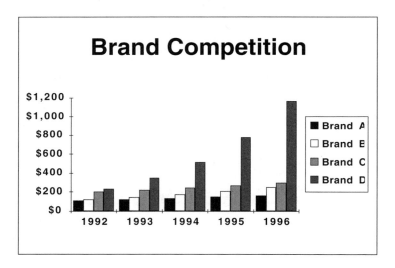

Scale

The scale is the numbering on the axes and should be in units that are easily understood by the viewers. Numbers rounded to whole numbers are mandatory on graphs for readability.

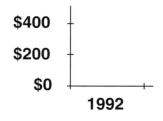

Software programs will typically set the high and low values based on the data entered. While this may be desired for many situations, for a graph series you should control the high and low amounts so all the graphs are displayed on the same relational scale.

Even if raw data is imported from another program with decimal values, you can easily adjust to whole numbers for display purposes.

X and Y Axes

The vertical line at the left is the Y axis; it is used for dollars, quantities, or volumes. This axis is the focus of the graph and represents a dependent variable that can be influenced or changed in some way by treatment.

Independent variables that cannot be controlled are placed on the horizontal line or the X axis. The X axis is frequently time data expressed in years, months, quarters, or weeks.

Grid

A grid shows scale and reference values. The grid may be displayed in squares like graph paper, which makes the quantity of the data reflected in the bars easier to interpret. Or, the grid may display only tick marks showing coordinates. You may prefer not to show a grid.

Tick Marks

Tick marks are coordinate marks on the grid used to help guide the viewer. Graphics programs will usually allow you to choose whether you want tick marks and, if you do, how frequently.

Labels

Many types of labels, or text annotation, can be included on a graph. Too many will confuse the viewer, but use enough to make the graph understandable. Labels can include a main title heading, a subtitle, and identification of the variables and parts of the graph. Consistent placement, either below or above the graph, is desirable; however, the most common placement of a label is usually above the displayed information.

Legend

A legend describes the symbols, shading, or color used on the graph. Most software programs allow you to specify whether or not you want to include the legend. Be sure the graph makes sense without the legend before deciding not to include it.

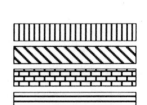

Special Effects

Special effects within your presentation graphs are possible through features of spreadsheet or graphics programs. The three main special effects are shading and color, exploding, and 3D.

Shading and Color

Sections of pie or bar charts can effectively use different shading patterns to help viewers distinguish different parts and compare differences. Color, rather than shading, is even more effective in highlighting different parts; however, shaded patterns in color are also possible with many programs. A pattern fill instead of color will usually produce a better appearance for handouts printed in black and white.

Exploding

Exploding the most important segment of a pie chart attracts attention to that part of the chart. Many graphics programs will allow you to explode the chart

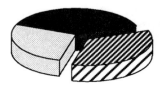

by moving one or more of the segments away from the rest of the pie.

3D

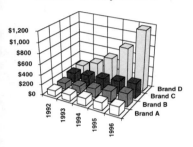

Brand Competition

An interesting effect of shadowing gives a three dimensional effect to graphs. A graphics program should have the option of performing this function. More sophisticated programs will allow you to key in the exact amount of depth and shading you desire. Be sure the look does not distract from the readability of the graph.

Pictorial Symbols

1995   2000

Bar charts may be enhanced by using pictorial symbols in place of the regular bars. To get the right proportions, you can use the software to construct the chart for accurate bar sizing. Make a temporary mark indicator to show the proper size of the bar, then delete the bars and place the pictorial symbols in the measured position.

Cautions

Use the same top value on the Y axis when comparing data on several charts or your data can be quite misleading or distorted.

Visual integrity is essential in constructing graphs. The information and statistics shown in a diagram or graph can reflect visual misinformation even though the graph is technically accurate.

For instance, assume you were using two graphs to show that several types of crime rates have decreased. For the Y values on one graph, 50 was the highest number of crimes; on the other graph, 100 was the highest. If you accepted the Y values the software gave you by default, the bars would be the same size. This like size would imply the same value, while the data actually reflects one amount twice as large as the other. Consistency is important when visually representing a series of related charts.

Finally, do not produce "chartjunk" by cluttering your diagrams or graphs. Have knowledgeable colleagues review your charts for both clarity and accuracy. A viewer should grasp the concept you are trying to illustrate quickly. The precise data is usually not as important as the general relationships. However, you could complement your presentation with a handout of detailed information if necessary.

With the background you have developed at this point, you are now ready to begin designing the visuals for your presentation. A total overview of visual design is presented in Chapter 6.

Graphs on your visuals should show only general ideas and relationships. If you want the audience to have more detailed information, make a handout.

Reference

Wiegner, Kathleen K. (October 15, 1990). "Data and Vision." *Forbes*, 93–95.

Designing Visuals

6

Your presentation can be enhanced by using graphic elements within the design of the visuals. Traditionally, professional graphic artists and typesetters were required to produce a visual including anything other than ordinary typewritten material. Today's computer-software packages allow presenters to incorporate a wide variety of visual enhancements without hiring typesetters and artists to do the work. Even though it is impossible to quickly absorb knowledge of artists and typographers, it is possible to follow sound principles of design.

Word-processing and desktop-publishing programs offer the advantages of large, bold fonts along with the incorporation of graphics. However, presentation software makes the visual preparation task much easier. For instance, the programs may include a dialog box asking whether a slide or an overhead size is desired. The size will then automatically adjust for your selection. Other helpful features include the capability of producing miniature visuals for handouts, making notes pages, and running computer-based slide shows.

Graphic Enhancements

Lines, borders, and boxes add interest to a visual and make it both eye-catching and pleasing to view. The

Designing the visuals is a task no longer limited to the traditional artist. With today's computer sophistication, the presenter using desktop-presentation software and clip art can easily incorporate artwork and special effects that only talented graphic artists could create in the past.

designer has complete control over colors used for each enhancement. Effective use of blank space is also important.

Rules

Rules come with a variety of choices and can be scaled (expanded or contracted) from very thin lines to very thick lines. They can be used to divide the visual into sections by placing a horizontal line between the title and the text or using vertical lines to divide the text into two or three columns.

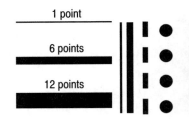

Boxes and Circles

Presentation software allows the user to draw squares, rectangles, or circles, using lines of different widths. A box is useful for enclosing either the title, the charts, or both. For an effective 3-D look, the boxes and circles can be made with a shadow box.

Borders and Frames

Using borders or frames around the entire visual is an alternative to include on a master template design. You can work logos, titles, and subtitles skillfully into the design of the border to keep this identification in front of the audience at all times. However, since slides are automatically inserted into a mount, and trans-parencies can be mounted, a frame or border around the edge is not essential. Thus, you can have more space available for designing the visual contents. If a frame is not used, identifying information should still be placed attractively in some way at the top or bottom of the visual.

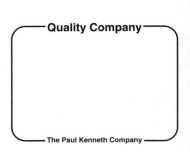

Blank Space

The effective use of blank space is an important part of all visuals. Too much information clutters a visual until the viewers either ignore the visual–because it is too complicated–or read it vigorously and forget to listen to the speaker. For the printed page, a desktop-publishing rule of thumb is that a page should have at least 50-percent blank space, which includes all margins and spacing between the various elements on the page. Visuals for projection should probably have as much as 60 or 70 percent of the space on the visual blank. This blank space should be evenly distributed unless your design purposely has an informal balance plan.

Shading and Backgrounds

10%

30%

60%

80%

Boxes, circles, or even whole visuals can be filled in by using a shading or screening effect–a gray shading. Most desktop-presentation, graphics, and drawing software can be screened from 0 to 100 percent to allow you to get the desired shade. In addition to a normal dot screening, most programs will have a variety of screening patterns from which you can choose.

Background designs are also available that can be imported. A company named Artbeats has a wide selection of designs, ranging from bricks, tiles, and line drawings to natural images such as water drops or flowers. These backgrounds can help set a theme. For instance, if you were displaying information about a spring fashion show, a flower or raindrop background might be appropriate. However, be careful to keep the background blends from overpowering the visual.

Typography

Individual letters, numbers, and symbols are type. With today's software, you have an enormous variety of options available to you in how you arrange and emphasize words with the use of type. You will need to make choices about many considerations–typefaces, type styles, type families, measurements, and other factors.

Typefaces/Fonts

The terms typeface and font are often used interchangeably. However, a *font* is a complete alphabet of uppercase and lowercase letters plus all related symbols, special characters, and punctuation marks. A *typeface* is the name of a particular font.

The entire appearance of a visual can be affected by the selection of typefaces. Characteristics such as formality and informality are expressed by typeface choices.

Two major categories of typefaces are serif and sans serif. *Serifs* are the short cross-strokes that project from the top or bottom of the main stroke of a letter.

Type without the serifs are called *sans serif*. (*Sans* means without.) An example of a sans serif type is Helvetica, which has a very clean appearance.

Some designers of visuals prefer the crisp, clean look of sans serif letters; others believe the serifs, particularly within the modern category, are more distinctive and, thus, are more readable when they are projected.

Try out different type fonts to get the readability and look you need. You may want to get opinions and

> Serif
>
> Sans Serif

reactions from several people before making your final selection. As a final caution on type fonts, be consistent and restrict yourself to one or two fonts within a single presentation.

Type Families

Helvetica
Helvetica Futura Heavy
Helvetica Compressed
N Helvetica Narrow
NB Helvetica Narrow Bold
NBI Helvetica Narrow Bold
Helvetica Oblique
LB Helvetica Black
L Helvetica Light

A type family is a variation of a typeface that shows a marked resemblance but has individual design variations in weight, proportion, angle, and surface texture. Though members of a typeface family may use varied and diverse type styles–such as bold, italics, or shadow–they all maintain the basic characteristics of the parent design. A type family can have as few as two members or as many as 40.

As in the case of typeface, restrict your use to two or three variations on a visual. Otherwise, your visual will look cluttered and will be confusing.

Type Styles

Helvetica
Helvetica Italic
Helvetica Bold
Helvetica Outline
Helvetica Shadow
HELVETICA ALL
CAPS
Helvetica StrikeThru

Frequently used type styles are: plain, bold, italic, underscore, shadow, and outline. However, many software programs have a variety of other selections, such as: word underline (versus all underline), strike-thru, small caps, all caps, superscript, subscript, and superior.

Type-style variations of a typeface should be used with care to serve their intended purpose. Too much variety on a visual can be distracting and confusing.

Type Size

Point size is the smallest typographic unit of measurement. One inch contains 72 points. A 12-point typeface measures 12 points from the top of the highest ascender (letters such as "h" or "l") to the end of the lowest descender (letters such as "p" or "y"). Line widths are also measured by points; thus, if you want a thin line, you might use 1 point; a medium-sized line, 4 points; and a thick line, 12 points.

Use large, bold type on visuals so information can be easily read. Use a hierarchy of sizes, with headings larger than the other text items in the visual. Appropriate typeface or font sizes for headings is between 24 and 36 points. Other text on the visual could appropriately be 18 to 24 points. Rarely should a font size below 14 points be used because it will not be visible from a distance.

(Note: Some presentation programs may use other measurements, such as centimeters. When using other measuring systems, be sure to follow the same idea of making headings and subheadings larger than the text in the body.)

Spacing

Both horizontal and vertical spacing should be considered in designing visuals for presentations. Horizontal spacing is called wordspacing, and vertical spacing is called either leading or linespacing.

Leading or Linespacing. Leading, commonly called linespacing, is the vertical space between lines. The term originated in the early days of typesetting when strips of lead were placed between rows of typeset letters on printing plates. This spreads the lines apart vertically for easier reading when printed.

Leading is measured from one baseline (the bottom of letters like "e" or "a") to the next line. If you are familiar with the typewriting term of single spacing,

7 pt
10 pt
11 pt
12 pt
14 pt
18 pt
24 pt
30 pt
36 pt
48 pt
60 pt
72 pt

the equivalent publishing term would be 12-point type on 12-point leading (12 on 12). Software provides automatic leading based on the size of the typeface being used. To increase the space between lines for easier reading, 12-point type could be adjusted with 13- or 14-point leading. Opening up lines is especially important when designing visuals for projection. The additional space really improves readability.

Too much leading, however, may make items appear unrelated. Test out your visuals for their readability when projected.

Wordspacing. Wordspacing refers to the space between words; it is automatically set in relation to the typeface and size selected. On a printed page, the closer that words are to each other, the easier they are to read–within reason. On a visual, words that are too close together may become harder to read. When you are using larger letters, you can add an extra space between letters in words.

An additional variation to horizontal spacing is *kerning*, which is adjusting the distance between individual letters in a word. The letters are usually brought closer together to make a better fit, such as an A and a V. Some software packages also use the term *tracking*–meaning the compressing or expanding of the space between the letters to make words easier to read.

Kerning and tracking procedures may help with readability as well as allow you flexibility in determining line lengths. Experiment to find the best combination for your selected typeface, size, and family.

Leading
Leading   12/12

Leading
Leading   12/14

Leading
Leading   12/18

Extra leading increases readability in designing visuals. However, too much leading also decreases readability.

AV AV AV
Wo Wo Wo

Tracking
Tracking
T r a c k i n g

Lowercase Versus Uppercase

As with many of today's publishing words, the terms lowercase and uppercase originated long ago when typesetters kept their capital letters in the upper case and small letters in the lower case. They would remove letters individually and set them in sequence to form words.

People often believe that using all caps makes a sign more readable or visible. One reason for this assumption is a carryover from typewriter days, when the only way to emphasize print was to make it appear larger with all-capital (uppercase) letters.

Actually, more than 95 percent of all reading material is in lowercase. Thus, people have not had as much practice reading uppercase letters as they have lowercase letters. The lack of descenders and ascenders in capital letters reduces readability, because capital letters are less distinctive at a quick glance.

Therefore, consider using lowercase with initial caps on your visuals—even on the titles. For emphasis, make titles large and bold. You want the viewer to read the visual quickly and easily.

ALL UPPERCASE LETTERS ARE HARD TO READ.

Words in lowercase letters are easier to read.

Enhancements

Interesting visual effects of stretching, distorting, and rotating text are possible. Software is available that will stretch words into a variety of unique shapes. Some draw programs can rotate or distort text, also. Many draw- and desktop-publishing programs can wrap blocks of text around irregular objects.

Though these interesting effects may be eye catching, use them with caution to be sure they add interest without too great a loss of readability. Try for an appealing combination.

Art as Design Elements

Have you ever picked up a book and thought of how boring it looked–though you had not read a single paragraph? People form judgments very quickly. The use of art can make your visuals draw the attention of your viewers much more readily. However, you should be extremely careful that the image your visuals portray will generate the type of emotional reaction you want.

Art for visuals can be obtained by three different methods: purchasing commercial art (called clip art); scanning artwork or photographs by using a scanner to digitize (read into a computer) the images; or using draw software to create your own art.

Clip Art

An abundance of clip art, frequently called *canned* art or symbols, is available for computer users. Most presentation software is packaged with some clip art. Clip art can be purchased separately by computer users. This canned art is typically delivered on disks with a hard-copy booklet of the images and their file names. Users buy the disk but, in effect, are paying for the right to use the clip art as many times as they wish.

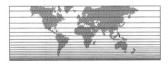

Clip art may be regular commercial software or either public domain or shareware. Regular commercial software is more expensive because the developer is trying to make a profit. They must pay artists for creating the work and also pay their company operating expenses.

Public-domain software is not copyrighted and is free to the public, although the supplier may charge a small fee to cover the costs of disks, mailing, and labor. Shareware has been donated or is shared by the creator rather than sold by a company. As with public-domain software, charges are needed to cover the administrative costs of copying and distributing the clip art. Shareware authors frequently include a message requesting that a small fee be sent if you find the software useful (an honor system).

Due to their larger storage capacity, compact disks and optical disks are used for clip art. Because of the large memory storage required for color line art and photography, the CD-ROM (read only memory) and optical disks are valuable peripheral devices to use.

On-line services through a modem are another method of obtaining clip art. Companies providing this service charge for each piece of clip art you request for your use. Clip art acquired on this basis from a commercial vendor can cost from $5 to $20 plus an annual subscription price for the service.

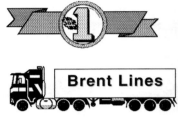

An abundance of clip art is available to help you illustrate key concepts or points.

Scanned Art

Using a scanner and special scanner software, you can digitize artwork, photographs, or text into computer-readable code. Most scanner software has functions that will allow you to manipulate, touch up, or alter the image. You also can import the digitized images into paint software for editing, before transferring the images into a presentation software for your presentation. With good editing features, you can produce a scanned image that is equal and sometimes better than the original. In addition, you can lighten or darken color shades, scale an image to the desired size, and even change a color.

Scanners are either gray-scale or color scanners; they are available in either sheet-fed or flatbed units.

Courtesy of Microtek Lab, Inc.

Scanned images have an upper resolution of 300 dots per inch–the same as most laser printers. Since scanner images take up to one megabyte of memory for 1 picture, a hard disk or removable cartridge is necessary.

The applications for scanned art are endless. A company logo, a photograph of a building or the company president, and drawings of a company's product line are all uses that could be made of a scanner. However, using art or photographs for scanning has legal considerations. You may not own the copyright to the image you are scanning. See the insert entitled "What's Legal, What's Not."

What's Legal, What's Not

The licensing agreement on most clip-art packages entitles you to use the art on one computer at a time and as part of any document or publication you choose to distribute. You don't normally have to identify the source of the art in a caption or print a copyright notice. Vendors understandably do, however, object to the sharing of clip art via a network in offices that haven't purchased a site license. Like any single-user program, clip-art disks should only be copied to make a backup or to transfer them to your hard disk.

"Piracy is a significant concern to clip-art manufacturers," says George Riddick, president of Marketing Graphics, Inc. "We want to give people the most flexibility in using images for what they do, but they should live up to the licensing agreement. We offer LAN and site license agreements. Early on, we had a copyright notice on our images, but it proved impractical. It's not our job to disrupt our customers' presentations."

J. Paul Grayson, chairman and CEO of Micrografx, is also trying to encourage licenses: "That way you can authorize a whole company to use it, and it can be placed on the hard disk server."

Some clip-art companies try to put a ceiling on the number of images you use per document. Envisions Solutions Technology, Burlingame, California, which sells the 200-piece Clip Art Collection ($49.95 or $24.95 with one of the company's hand scanners) says you can use up to 11 images per document. "You have to get our permission for more than that," says David Schulhof, Envisions president. The fear is that someone might try to resell the art.

Though clip art can be transferred from a Macintosh to an IBM-compatible computer, clip art companies say a version should only be used in the environment for which the disk was purchased. If you do otherwise, "you'd be breaking our agreement since you can only use it on one computer at a time," says Steve Schoolman, president of Computer Application Resources, Inc. "From a practical standpoint, we probably wouldn't care."

There's also the question of taking a publication, with clip art included, to a service bureau for high-resolution output. Should the service bureau have purchased its own copy of the clip art? According to Schoolman, the answer is no. "We give our users the freedom to use the art in any kind of publication they want. We see them as reprinting their entire publication—not just our art. Otherwise, we would have a severe copy protection problem."

Scanning technology creates its own legal pitfalls: While material appearing in government-issued bulletins, including charts and graphs, is almost always in public domain, users with access to scanners need to be careful about appropriating art from copyrighted sources of any kind. Technically, the publisher of copyrighted source material has to grant permission for any licit reproduction. A credit line and/or a fee is often involved. You're talking a major risk when "borrowed" art appears in any publication circulated outside the office, especially if it is used in a way that could be construed as promotional. Copyright lawyers live for this.

—M.A., *Personal Computing,* August, 1990

User-Created Art

Rather than purchasing clip art or scanning images from artwork or photographs, some people like to create their own art using paint, draw, or some presentation software. Then, they do not have to worry about another speaker using the same piece of clip art or violating copyright laws.

A variety of programs are available for creating original art with the computer. Such programs come equipped with tool boxes containing items commonly found on an artist's workstation—pens, paintbrushes, paint buckets, spray cans, color palettes, line/box/circle tools, etc. Textured patterns and color templates allow interesting effects to be added. Original production of art can be very rewarding for artistically inclined people. It can be quite time consuming, also.

> Draw programs such as the following can help you create your own art.
> Adobe Illustrator
> Aldus Freehand
> Canvas
> CorelDraw
> DrawPerfect
> MacDraw

General Design Principles

After examining graphic design devices, type, and art, a few general design principles are important in obtaining an effective overall look to your visuals.

Landscape Versus Portrait

Basic design principles involved in page layout for desktop publishing apply to designing visuals—with one major difference. Visuals for transparencies and 35 mm slides should be designed using *landscape* (horizontal) versus *portrait* (vertical) placement.

Most people automatically begin to make their visuals using portrait arrangement simply because that is how text is usually printed on paper for word

Landscape

Portrait

processing and desktop publishing. Yet, as a general design principle, a landscape arrangement should be used for three reasons.

First, the eye finds it more pleasing to look across rather than down and up–a soothing feeling like looking at a wide view of the horizon with blue skies and spreading clouds. Second, longer lines are available for bullet lists and pictures when the visual is wider. The last reason is simply because the bottom of a vertically designed visual may not be clearly viewed in most room arrangements.

A landscape format should normally be used for visuals.

Alignment

Alignment refers to how the text lines up on the margins or within the center. Consistent alignment throughout the presentation contributes to unity and continuity.

Left. Alignment of text for a flush left and ragged right edge will result in varying line lengths. Effort should be made to space the words so a minimum amount of variation occurs. Hyphenation may be used on occasion if absolutely necessary, but it should be used with extreme care to assure readability.

A slight difference in line length gives copy a distinctive and perhaps less formal look. It can even increase legibility by anchoring the eye movement from line to line. Therefore, left alignment is frequently a good choice to use in making visuals.

Right. In right alignment, the lines are uneven on the left but align flush on the right margin. This arrangement is appropriate with only a few lines of type and when you may want to draw interest to the material on the end of the lines.

Centered. A formal and conservative alignment method is centering each line. Both the left and right margins will be ragged. Even though the visual may have a look of dignity, viewers may have trouble reading centered lines as easily. Centered lines are more difficult to read because the viewer must find the beginning of each new line. Therefore, use of centered lines should be limited to visuals with no more than two or three lines.

Justified. When all lines are the same length and begin and end at the same positions, text is justified. Justification should not be used if wide gaps are between words or if the type appears to become smaller or larger when justified. Since justification works better with long lines than short lines, it may not be a good choice for visuals when large font sizes are used.

Balance

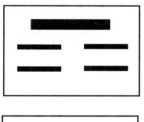

Balance is created by placing all the elements on a visual to achieve a general sense of equilibrium—so visuals do not appear lopsided. Formal balance involves placing the art and type in a centered manner, and reflects formality and dignity. For informal balance, images are placed at random (but with an informal balance plan) on the visual. This type of balance is generally more interesting and eye catching than formal balance, and provides much more flexibility in design.

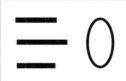

Proportion

As mentioned earlier, blank space improves readability. However, this blank space should be arranged into pleasing proportions. Space around the edges and within the visual itself is extremely important.

Artwork and text should be sized or scaled appropriately to fit the allocated space. Most presentation programs can adjust image and text dimensions for a pleasing appearance.

Sequence

One method of sequencing a design capitalizes on the natural eye movement when reading. Through habit, the eye moves from left to right and from top to bottom in a "Z" pattern when first scanning a page. Therefore, the first area a viewer will see is the upper left-hand corner of the visual. Placing the presentation title in this corner would give the viewer a constant reminder of what the presentation topic is; or, you might want your company logo in that position to remind the audience what company you represent. Since the last area to be viewed is the lower right-hand corner, you might prefer to place your name there.

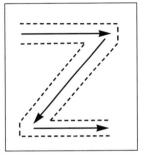

The "Z" pattern is a common layout system.

Emphasis

One element of the visual should dominate all others. This dominating element could be the title, the art, or the message itself. Both color and size are effective tools to use in creating the dominant feature of the visual. How to use color effectively will be discussed in Chapter 7.

Unity

A unifying design, shape, and pattern should hold the visuals together within a presentation. Therefore, the

Limit elements–such as type, color, artwork–to two or three selections of each.

design of the master template is very important. You should follow a theme within a presentation rather than giving an audience the feeling of "Wow, what will the speaker show next?" As important as the design is, it should almost be considered transparent and should blend in with the talk rather than be a show stealer.

The next chapter is devoted to the use of color in presentations. Color can add a whole new dimension to your presentation–whether the color consideration is your room, the visuals, or even your handouts.

Reference

Antonoff, Michael. (August, 1990). "Picture This." *Personal Computing*, 100.

Working with Color

Today's technology makes it possible to use color in designing presentations—with the potential of selecting 16.8 million colors. Of course, color output devices—printers, projection units, or film recorders—are needed to make use of these colors in your presentation.

Since using color can greatly increase your production costs, you may need justification for this added expenditure. A summary of research findings on the effectiveness of color is given at the end of this chapter.

Within visuals, color can be used for coding purposes, for affecting the presentation mood, and for improving readability. Certain combinations work better than others.

Coding/Signaling

Color is a useful coding or signaling tool to show either association or differentiation. It can show emphasis or hierarchies, too.

Association or Differentiation

Colors create identity. For instance, the color green means money or go; yellow says caution; red means stop or danger. Developing an effective color scheme for a presentation can establish a similar identity—

Henry Ford thought no one would want anything but a basic black car. He was wrong! Today's world is a multi-colored one. People are no longer satisfied with black-and-white cars, photographs, movies, television, or newspapers. The real world is full of color images—not monochrome. In this chapter, you will find ideas for choosing the right colors for your presentation.

although the associations may be different from those mentioned above. For instance, if you are developing a motivational speech, you might want to use red in your background theme throughout the presentation to show a high level of intensity—with the interpretation of *go for it* rather than stop. In contrast, a yellow background would give a cheery light touch to the presentation—not caution.

Color is useful in distinguishing between elements. Handouts using different colors of paper can help the audience to find a particular sheet quickly—for instance, "on the blue sheet . . . ." Illustrations on the visuals (and handouts, if a color printer is available) can be done in color to distinguish different classes, elements, or levels.

> Color coding your handouts can help the audience find a particular handout quickly.

Emphasis or Hierarchies

You can draw attention to type or graphics in your visual by using a dark, vivid color on a light background or a light color on a dark background. For example, in using a dark blue background, white can be the most dominating color (useful for the title), followed by a bright yellow for a bullet list. Both white and yellow stand out; since white contrasts more, the reader's eye will travel to the white title because it will dominate over the yellow list.

Hierarchies, showing either a logical progression or level of importance, can be indicated by using colors going from either light to dark or gray to bright. In contrast, a rainbow progression gives equal importance to all items.

Mood Effects/Color Psychology

Color sets a mood. It can set a style, also. Mood effects and color psychology should be carefully considered as you design a presentation to create the effect you desire for your message.

In the following insert, Dr. Stephen Mason, a psychologist in Irvine, California, summarizes many of the psychological theories on color, which you should consider in selecting colors for your presentation visuals. If you set up a meeting or training room, consider these color theories as you develop the environmental design.

Law enforcement officials in a number of cities around the country have come to a rather startling conclusion: Color can help to subdue certain prisoners. Placed in an all-pink room and observed through a two-way mirror, difficult detainees have been observed to calm way down. I've learned to wear a pink shirt when returning a purchase to the department store and don't have all the tags and receipts. Friends in sales have confided that they wear pink as a means of quickly fatiguing customer resistance.

There are many reported instances of specific hues influencing specific behaviors. Color plays a role in how we think, feel, and act.

In presentations, the trick is to use color as one might use musical notes. Variety is important. As with an orchestral score, it's the blend of high notes, low notes, and tempo that keep people interested. Make it all loud and you have a boiler factory. Make it all quiet and you have people nodding off. Mix colors for emphasis or to affect mood.

Red seems to be a color that demands attention. Yellow is easier to spot (note the increased number of yellow hunting jackets, life vests, and emergency vehicles), but red still says, "This is important, so pay attention." In presentations, use red sparingly.

Yellow will get an audience's attention, too, but their mood will be slightly different. Where red demands attention, yellow says "Hey! Hey! Look at this. It's really great." Yellow is an optimistic color–cheerful and sunny. During a presentation, save yellow for important information that you want assimilated in a positive way.

Use pink if you simply want to present a message and then get away with an absolute minimum of hassle. They don't call it a "Pink Slip" for nothing! Pink just seems to take the fight out of people.

Blue puts everyone in a quiet and tranquil mood. If you are expecting a problem with the air conditioning, use pale blue background, as it will make people think a room is three or four degrees cooler than it actually is.

Finally, if you want to bring out some creative interaction, use violet. For some reason, this color has the ability to make otherwise conservative people soar in flights of fantasy. It's also the most popular color of adolescents and those among us who love romance novels. But too much violet may bring on a meditative state–like anchovies, a little violet goes a long way.

–Dr. Stephen Mason (December, 1989)
"Seeing Red? Feeling Blue?", *Data Training*

Pink just seems to take the fight out of people.

Readability

For the psychology of color to be effective, however, visuals must be legible. Poor color choices and combinations can hinder rather than help. Try out color visuals to see if they are readable–especially from a distance.

As a word of caution in selecting color combinations, remember that approximately ten percent of the male population and almost .5 percent of the female population are color impaired and may have trouble distinguishing between colors such as red and green. Therefore, they would have trouble interpreting a graph using red and green side by side. They might see one large area rather than two different areas.

Color Definitions

Color is fundamental to virtually every facet of life. Yet, the way one individual perceives a color may be different from another individual's perception.

If colored lights in the light primaries of red, green, and blue are projected in overlapping circles, they mix to form the secondary colors of yellow, magenta, and cyan. Where all three primaries overlap, the result is the color white. This system is called additive color and is used in computer graphics and color television.

Colors seen on objects operate in a different system than the system seen in beams of light. In this type of system, the result of the three primary colors overlapping is the color black. This method is the one used in printing processes.

Other elements useful in understanding color are hue, saturation, lightness, and brightness. In computer graphics, another element is graduated color.

With additive color, the overlap at the center is white.

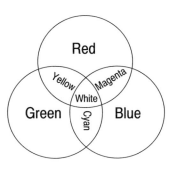

Hue

Hue refers to the actual color of an object. An object is red, blue, green, yellow, and so on. The perception of hue is affected by background or surrounding colors. For instance, a red object placed on a white background will look different when it is placed on a black background. The hue and perception of size will be affected.

Saturation

Saturation refers to the vividness of the hue–it could also be referred to as value. Colors can have different saturation levels or amounts of color. Yellow appears to be less saturated than blue.

Lightness

Lightness refers to the degree of lightness or darkness in a color, depending on how much white, gray, or black is in the color. The effect of white in a color makes it appear lighter; black added will make the same color appear darker.

Brightness

Brightness refers to intensity. The amount of brightness of a color can vary depending upon the amount of lighting. Pure white represents maximum brightness; pure black represents the minimum brightness.

Graduated Colors

Many computer programs using color can produce special effects–called graduated, gradient, or ramped–within colors dissolving into interesting blends. One color, two colors, or a whole range of colors can be selected. Color ramping may be specified as vertical, horizontal, diagonal right, diagonal left, from corner, or from title.

The use of graduated colors can provide an interesting, appealing background for your master template. Some programs will allow objects or text to be filled with graduated color. However, be sure the colors do not distract or reduce readability.

The three inserts by Suzanne M. Topping included in the following pages list ideas for using color for Symbolism of Color Groups, Conveying Themes Through Color, and Choosing Color. Refer to these lists when you are deciding on colors for your presentation.

Symbolism of Color Groups

Festive

Light Saturated Colors: These vivid colors convey lively, festive moods. They are energetic colors which enliven drab pieces. They are best used as accents.

Dignified

Dark Saturated Colors: Carry a sense of dignity, richness, and elegance.

Cheery

Light Unsaturated Colors: Created by adding white to saturated colors; they are also known as tints. When mixed with large amounts of white, saturated colors become pastels, known for their soft, cheery, or dreamy qualities.

Soft

Saturated colors mixed with small amounts of white may appear washed out or dull, therefore weaker in symbolism than their saturated parents.

Dull/Rich

Dark Unsaturated Colors: Created by adding black to saturated colors.

Black added to dark, saturated colors tends to strengthen them, reinforcing themes of richness and elegance. The addition of black makes colors heavier and more serious, even to the point of becoming stern or melancholy.

Dull or Muddy Colors: Created by adding both black and white to saturated colors.

When both white and black are added to a saturated color, the color loses its vibrancy and becomes neutral or even drab. Dull colors can rarely carry themes on their own; they need support from more vibrant colors, or should be used as backgrounds. Dull colors by themselves tend to become depressing.

–Suzanne M. Topping (1990)
Graphic Design and Color in Today's Office
Eastman Kodak Company

Reprinted with permission of Eastman Kodak Company.

Conveying Themes Through Color

When you combine colors creatively, you can portray themes, convey ideas, and stimulate your viewers to take action.

The information below is categorized by theme, and offers some ideas for creating the moods you may need to project. Use these suggestions to help form your own ideas and themes.

Cleanliness: Use combinations of white and blue or white and green to create crisp, clean, or pure images. Packaging of most bathroom cleansers, bleaches, first-aid products, and toothpastes use these colors to project a squeaky-clean and sanitary image.

Cleanliness

Coldness: Create a cold color scheme by using cool colors: tints of blue, green, gray, and purple. Be careful when including any warm colors because they will take away from the chill of the piece.

Coldness

Depth

Distance or Depth: Create an impression of depth or distance by gradually moving from light colors (near) to dark colors (far). You can use different colors or shades of the same color.

You can also create depth by placing warm-colored images on cool-colored backgrounds. The warm-colored images will appear closer to the viewer.

Elegance

Elegance: Two-color combinations of gold, silver, black, white, red, brown, and navy blue create the feel of elegance. The combination of black, gold, and white appears particularly expensive.

Excitement

Excitement: To generate excitement, combine red with bright, unusual secondary colors like magenta, orange, and chartreuse. Some of these combinations clash, which enhances the excitement. Black can be added to help ease vibrating effects and increase contrast, an important element in exciting designs.

Femininity

Femininity: Femininity was once conveyed with whites, soft colors, and frills. You can also use pinks, purples, and valentine shades that have been added to the list.

Technology

High-Tech: The look of the high-tech age is achromatic and highly contrasting. Use a basic palette of white, black, and shades of gray, and include sparks of vivid color to add interest.

Luxury

Luxury: Create a feeling of affluence by using the traditional colors signifying wealth and luxury: rich reds, golds, purples, and black.

Masculinity

Masculinity: Portray masculinity with combinations of red with browns, black, and nature tones to conjure images of leather, the outdoors, and strength.

Naturalness

Naturalness: Earth tones, especially tans, browns, and off-whites, should predominate in pieces with a natural theme. Earthy reds, greens, and purples can also be used. Natural colors tend to be composite mixtures rather than pure, simple colors. You may want to include a small amount of a brighter natural color like blue or green to keep the piece from becoming visually tedious.

Romance: Mimic spring colors and play up pink tones for an innocent feeling of romance. Use valentine shades to create a feeling of passionate romance; pink to denote softness, purple to symbolize passion, red to convey heat. Adding white to red makes the passion playful, adding black makes it sinful.

Romance

Seasonality: To portray the feel of spring, summer, fall, or winter, use the colors of those seasons. Spring-like designs should include pale greens, purples, pinks, and yellows. To create summer's sunniness, add white to brightened versions of spring's colors and bright blues. You can also lend a summery feeling by using the traditional colors of summer clothing, like nautical red, white, and blue. For an impression of fall, choose the colors of autumn leaves and the harvest: browns, rust, tan, pine green, golden orange, and deep yellow. The cool colors of white, blue, green, and purple carry a winter theme best.

Seasonality

Tranquility: Reverse the principles for creating exciting designs and you will have guidelines for tranquil pieces. Use pale, cool colors, grays, and secondary shades (which tend to be more tranquil than primary colors). Keep contrast to a minimum to limit excitement.

Tranquility

Violence: Combinations of red and black are often used to create a violent feeling; since black symbolizes death, and red symbolizes anger and action, you can see why. Think about the packaging of items like cans of insecticide, suspense novels, heavy-metal albums, and horror-movie posters.

Violence

Warmth: Create a warm color scheme by using warm colors. Use reds, oranges, and yellows if you want to project HOT! Stick to oranges, yellows, and warm browns to turn down the heat a little. If you need to include cooler colors like blue, green, or gray, warm them up by adding yellow (to blue or green) or red (to gray).

Warmth

Youth

Youth: Since young people's tastes change so quickly, the best way to project a youthful spirit is to watch what is currently in style and follow its lead.

Portray infancy and early childhood by using the stereotypical baby colors: pastel shades of pink, blue, yellow, and the newer blue-green. Combining these colors with white carries the viewer straight back to the nursery.

–Suzanne M. Topping (1990)
Graphic Design and Color in Today's Office
Eastman Kodak Company

Reprinted with permission of Eastman Kodak Company.

Choosing Colors

Don't use too many colors. Remember: less is more. A common mistake, especially of people new to designing with color, is to include so many colors that they achieve only discord. Be careful not to use combinations of too many vivid colors; think about limiting vivids to accent areas.

Select object colors after choosing a background. Pick the color for the largest area first, then think about the smaller areas. If the subject matter dictates your selection of accent color, choose a background that is compatible and that creates harmony. For example, if you are designing an ad for Florida oranges, you might want to use sunshine yellow and orange as accents, with a darker color as background.

Select hues after deciding on overall lightness levels. Mood is conveyed more by lightness level than by hue, so making your color selections in order of lightness, then hue, allows you to think of the overall mood first. If you choose a wide range of hues but use them all in the same shade, the piece will be dull. Selecting different tints and tones within the same hue, however, can create a lively piece. A combination of pale pink, vermilion, maroon, and magenta, for example, would be eye-catching to say the least! Contrast is needed to add visual interest.

When in doubt, go achromatic. If you are having difficulty selecting colors or limiting your colors, think about using a palette of black, white, and gray. You can also make one of these shades a major player in your piece along with your chromatic colors.

Think carefully before using trendy, cliche'd, or overused colors. You may not get attention if the viewer has seen the color combination too often.

If you want to create a very up-to-date color combination using colors that are on the cutting edge of popular use, try looking through copies of fashion magazines. The fashion colors shown in these publications tend to move into popular usage for other areas of design.

Colors look bolder when used in large areas. Tone down the saturation and contrast levels when dealing with large spaces. Conversely, when reducing the size of a large colored area or image, you may need to adjust the color to improve its vibrancy.

Warm colors generally work best in small areas on cooler, more subdued backgrounds.

Use black in combination with two other colors for a striking, rich composition.

Avoid reds and greens with low saturation levels because your piece may be viewed by people who are red-green colorblind.

> –Suzanne M. Topping (1990)
> *Graphic Design and Color in Today's Office*
> Eastman Kodak Company

Reprinted with permission of Eastman Kodak Company.

Color Research

Research has shown that color enhances the communication process. Green (1984) concludes that color:

(1) accelerates learning, retention, and recall by 55 to 78 percent;

(2) improves and increases comprehension up to 73 percent;

(3) increases willingness to read up to 80 percent;

(4) increases recognition up to 78 percent;

(5) increases motivation and participation up to 80 percent;

(6) reduces error count from 55 to 35 percent;

(7) sells (products and ideas) more effectively by 50 to 85 percent.

His conclusions were based on two different studies. The first was by the Bureau of Advertising on *Color in Newspaper Advertising in the Top 100 Markets.* The second study was by Xerox Corporation, who commissioned the management consultant firm of Case & Company, Inc., to verify the significance of using color in print. They did this by testing and interviewing business executives and university students.

Numerous other studies have also found that using color in the presentation of either written or oral communications contributes to its effectiveness. Lamberski (1982) found that color-coded presentational materials were superior to black and white. Color-coding had a more positive impact on visual than on verbal task tests.

Berry (1982) tested an instructional unit about the human heart using slides and an audiotape. His

Using color in print makes a difference.

Color-coded presentation materials were found to be superior to black and white.

research design included treatment groups using different types of visual illustration: black-and-white shaded drawings, realistic color drawings, or non-realistic color drawings. The realistic color group obtained higher achievement, although the differences disappeared after six weeks.

> Groups using realistic color obtained higher initial achievement.

Seddon and Shubber (1984) investigated use of overhead transparencies containing a sequence of diagrams to represent a three-dimensional structure at different stages during a rotation. Significantly more learning occurred when the transparencies contained multi-colored diagrams exposed simultaneously or individually in a cumulative manner.

> More learning occurred with multi-colored diagrams.

Hativa and Reingold (1987) experimented with the effectiveness of two versions of computer software used as an electronic blackboard to present geometric concepts to ninth-grade students. The experimental version incorporated color, animation, and nonverbal sounds as stimuli, and the no-stimulus version was displayed in monochrome. Both immediate and delayed learning were significantly better for the experimental group.

> Using color, animation, and nonverbal sounds as stimuli resulted in improvements for both immediate and delayed learning.

Gremillion and Jenkins (1981) conducted a study to examine the effects of color-coded transparencies on information retention from a lecture. Color was used to emphasize distinctions and relationships in the information content. The findings showed a significant improvement in recall when color was used in a comprehension and learning task.

> Significant improvement in recall was found when color was used in a comprehension and learning task.

Benbasat, Dexter, and Todd (1986) conducted a series of lab experiments to examine the joint and individual effects of color and graphics within the context of different user characteristics and task settings. The decision-making task setting was chosen

In decision-making tasks, color affects performance measures and user preferences.

Color improves time performance for extracting information from graphs.

Black and white pictures are equally as dramatic as color pictures in war tragedy scenes.

Dyslexic readers do better with blue or gray plastic overlays.

specifically to require the use of judgment rather than recall or search-and-locate. The authors found that color affected performance measures and user preferences; they also noted an interaction between personality and color.

Hoadley (1990) conducted laboratory experiments to study the effects of color on a decision maker's ability to extract information from different graphical and tabular presentations. The results indicated that color improves time performance for extracting information from tables, pie charts, and bar graphs, and accuracy performance for pie charts and line graphs.

On the other hand, one experiment by Michael Williams (1989) examined news photographs in stories related to the Vietnam War. He found color pictures appearing in *Life Magazine* were not regarded as any more violent than the black and white pictures. The black and white pictures were equally dramatic in relating the war tragedy scenes.

Another study by researcher Mary C. Williams (1990), who holds a doctorate in psychology and specializes in the study of visual factors contributing to reading disability, found that colored plastic overlays–particularly blue and gray–used on books can produce immediate and dramatic effects on the reading performance of children who are reading disabled or dyslexic. In fact, all readers did better with the plastic overlays (Miller, 1990).

The effects of color also apply to more than the presentation media. Many of the color theories can also be applied to the presentation environment. Other aspects of the environment are considered in the next chapter.

References

Benbasat, I.; Dexter, A. S.; and Todd, P. (1986). "The Influence of Color- and Graphical-Information Presentation in a Managerial-Decision Simulation." *Human Computer Interaction.*

Berry, Louis H. (1982). "An Exploratory Study of the Relative Effectiveness of Realistic and Non-Realistic Color in Visual Instructional Materials." Paper presented to *Educational Communications and Technology*, Dallas, TX. (From *ERIC Abstracts*, 1/83 to 9/90, Document Reproduction Service No. ED 223 194)

Green, Ronald E. (October, 1984). "The Persuasive Properties of Color." *Marketing Communications*, 50-54.

Gremillion, L. L., and Jenkins, A. A. (1981). "The Effects of Color-Enhanced Information Presentations." *Proceedings of the Second International Conference on Information Systems,* Cambridge, MA.

Hartley, James. (Spring, 1987). "Designing Electronic Text: The Role of Print-Based Research." *Educational Communications and Technology, 35.* (From *ERIC Abstracts,* 1/83 to 9/90, Document Reproduction Service No. EJ 363 802)

Hativa, Nira, and Reingold, Aliza. (1987). "Effects of Audiovisual Stimuli on Learning Through Microcomputer-Based Class Presentation." *Instructional Science, 18.* (From *ERIC Abstracts,* 1/83 to 9/90, Document Reproduction Service No. EJ 363 864)

Hoadley, Ellen D. (February, 1990). "Investigating the Effects of Color." *Communications of the Association for Computing Machinery, 33,* 120-125, 129.

Lamberski, Richard J. (1982). "The Instructional Effect of Color in Immediate and Delayed Retention." Paper presented to *Educational Communications and Technology,* Dallas, TX. (From *ERIC Abstracts,* 1/83 to 9/90, Document Reproduction Service No. ED 223 201)

Mason, Stephen. (December, 1989). "Seeing Red? Feeling Blue?" *Data Training,* 28-29.

Miller, Sue. (December 14, 1990). "One Simple Device Helps Dyslexics to Read Better." *Los Angeles Times,* E24.

Seddon, G. M., and Shubber, K. E. (1984). "The Effects of Presentation Mode and Colour in Teaching the Visualisation of Rotation in Diagrams of Molecular Structures." *Research in Science and Technological Education, 2.* (From *ERIC Abstracts,* 1/83 to 9/90, Document Reproduction Service No. EJ 309 085)

Topping, Suzanne M. (1990). *Graphic Design and Color in Today's Office.* Eastman Kodak Company, 14, 18-20, 23-24.

Williams, M. Michael. (1989). "News Photographs in Stories Related to Vietnam: A Content Analysis of Photographs Relating to the Vietnam War, Appearing in *Life Magazine* from January 1, 1966, Through

February 28, 1970." Paper presented to Association for Education in Journalism and Mass Communication, Washington, DC. (From *ERIC Abstracts,* 1/83 to 9/90, Document Reproduction Service No. ED 311 505)

Zelanski, Paul, and Fisher, Mary Pat. (1989). *Color.* Englewood Cliffs, New Jersey: Prentice Hall.

Considering the Environment

If you are an invited speaker on a conference or convention program, you may have little or no opportunity to provide input on the presentation environment. You may be only one of many speakers who will be using the facility in a particular day.

Hopefully, someone has been responsible for choosing the best arrangement for all and has also tried to meet each speaker's individual needs. If possible, visit the room and become comfortable with the surroundings and the equipment before you present.

A good meeting coordinator will prepare for you and your presentation needs. This coordinator will contact you before your presentation, either by telephone or mail, to find out your equipment needs and special requirements.

If you have not been contacted, you should take the initiative to find out if the equipment or room arrangements you need will be available. When equipment or room arrangements cannot be made available to fit your needs, you have a choice of either providing the equipment yourself or changing your presentation to fit in with whatever equipment is or will be available.

If you are the only speaker or a specially featured speaker, you may be able to have more input into

This chapter analyzes the physical environment for giving a presentation. Factors examined include the general location, the facility itself, and ergonomic factors within the room.

arranging the presentation environment. This chapter assumes you are able to have full input into your presentation environment.

Even though you do not always have this privilege, you need to be aware of the ideal presentation environment. Perhaps you can make minor changes, even if you cannot select and change the entire setting.

The first step consists of choosing a location. Then, you need to consider specific facility arrangements, including the speaking or stage area, the audience seating area, and ergonomic factors of the facility.

Location of the Presentation

Realtors have an expression about buying real estate—"the three most important factors are location, location, and location." If you are going to be presenting an all-day seminar and want to attract an audience, you also need to consider location, location, and location.

You need to choose an area convenient for people as well as one where people want to go. If most people are flying in from other cities, a location near the airport would be convenient. For this reason, many hotels locate near airports. Places with special entertainment attractions may also be an enticing factor in trying to draw attendance. When the seminar is an ideal vacation spot, the idea of a combination business trip and vacation is appealing and may attract more participants.

If the people attending are commuting from a local area, you need to consider places convenient for the

> The choice of location for your presentation can make a difference. If you are arranging a seminar, choose a convenient as well as an enticing location.

largest number of people attending. Be sure adequate parking is available.

Since the location of a meeting or seminar can reflect on the speaker or the organization sponsoring the speaker, you want to choose a location accordingly. If you want to convey a sense of success, you would not want to choose a location in a rundown part of town.

Most large hotels have conference and convention rooms available. They will provide for the rental of audiovisual equipment, or they should be able to provide you with companies in the area where you can rent such equipment. Be sure you understand how these services are handled.

In engaging the facility, you need to be aware of internal as well as external factors. Are eating establishments in the area adequate, and where are they? Where are the restrooms? Are pay phones near the room? Are water fountains available?

The Presentation Facility

The facility for a presentation involves a look at the stage or speaking area and the audience or seating area. In addition, available break or social areas are also important.

The stage area refers to the area where you will be during the presentation. Good eye contact with a speaker is necessary to maintain audience interest.

If you are in a large room or auditorium, you may find a raised platform or stage is provided. This elevation is helpful in allowing an audience to have a better view of you, the speaker. In smaller room settings, you may find you have closer contact with the audience by being in front on the same level as the audience.

Lectern

In either the auditorium or room-type setting, usually a lectern is available. A lectern may be as simple as a plywood box, useful for propping up notes, or as complex as an electronic command post to control lighting, screens, and projectors.

Use a lectern as a device to assist you in your presentation. Be careful it does not become a shield hiding you from the audience. You do not want to appear frozen in place, clutching the lectern as a barrier.

Microphone

A microphone may be a part of the lectern or on a stand by itself. Do not be afraid of a microphone! Many speakers shy away from microphones and will ask an audience if they can be heard in the back. How can people say yes or no if they cannot hear the question?

In addition, simply being heard is not enough. Your voice should be loud and clear to easily penetrate the minds of all the audience members. If possible, test a microphone before your actual presentation to get used to how you sound with your voice amplified and to be sure the system is working properly.

A large percentage of people have some hearing impairment; however, all people will listen more attentively if they can easily hear your words. People with hearing impairments may hear your voice adequately but have trouble discriminating your words. Remember to watch your audience and use interactive techniques (such as asking for feedback by a show of hands or by verbal responses) to make sure the audience is with you.

Projection Screen

Several factors are important concerning projection screens. You need to consider the size, the type of surface, and whether a front or rear projection method is used.

Sizes. According to Minnesota Western Visual Presentation Systems, the optimum screen size should be related to the seating capacity of the room. The size can be very easily determined by using the following formulas.

✔ Two times the screen height should equal the distance from the screen to the first row of seats.

✔ Six times the screen width should equal the distance from the screen to the last row of seats.

✔ A distance of four feet from the bottom of the screen to the floor should be allowed for unobstructed viewing by the audience.

Surface Types. Projection screens may be as simple as a white or light-colored wall (if nothing else is available) or a variety of specially-made materials. Screen surfaces can be classified into three types: matte, glass beaded, or pearlescent.

A *matte surface* is an all-purpose type of screen for overhead projection or a variety of forms of projection. This type of screen, whether on a wall or pull-down screen, is frequently found, as it is less expensive than the other types.

A screen with a *glass beaded surface* contains millions of optical-quality spherical glass beads that provide superior brightness, greater picture depth, richer detail, and excellent tone graduation in a normally darkened room. This screen surface is recommended for slide or movie projection and offers about three times the screen brightness of a matte surface. Viewing angles are limited to a total seating cone of 60 degrees.

A *pearlescent* screen, useful for video and LCD projection, has excellent reflectivity and increased brilliance without loss of image sharpness or registration. A direct computer-to-projector system can be used with a ceiling-mounted projection unit. These units contain multiple lenses for color projection and can be controlled by remote controls and/or a computer. A list of available products and supplies is in the appendix. Regular VCR tapes can be shown through these systems. Thus, the quality of the screen is very important for good viewing.

Screens may be portable or permanently built into the room design. Portable screens may offer more flexibility in determining where you want the screen, where you will position yourself, etc. However, portable screens are usually smaller and may not have the superior projection material of a screen that is permanently built into the room design.

Front or Rear Projection. Projection may be either front or rear projection. The terms refer to whether the projection equipment is located in the room itself or in a control room behind the speaking area and not visible to the audience.

Front projection consists of placing the projector in the room with the lens focused directly on the projection screen at the front of the room. The placement of the projection equipment will depend upon the type of equipment and the particular lens used. Slide projector lenses range from one-inch to 14-inch lenses. Try out your particular equipment in the presentation environment to determine the proper placement.

A slide projector can also be placed in a booth or separate room at the very back of the room. The room will have a glass window or be equipped with special holes for the lens to project to the screen in the front of the room.

In rear projection, the slide projector is placed in an area or room behind the speaker. Mirrors are used to reverse the images and reflect a right-reading image on the screen in the front of the room.

A special projection room–whether in the front or the back of the room–increases construction costs; however, such projection is considered more professional with several advantages.

✔ The noise and heat of the projector will not be evident since the projector is housed in a separate area.

✔ More overall lighting is possible, making it easier for the audience to see the presenter and take notes.

✔ The speaker can stand in front of the screen without casting a shadow on the projected image.

Audience Seating for the Presentation

Arrangements for audience seating will be affected by the space available. Therefore, you should be aware of various possibilities and their benefits. Both the speaker and the projection screen should be clearly visible by all members of the audience. However, the screen should not dominate over the speaker. A description of a variety of audience-seating methods is given next. The illustrations in the diagrams show suggested audience seating arrangements.

Auditorium or Theater

Chairs are placed in rows with center and/or side aisles. The chairs face the stage or speaking area. More people can be accommodated with this arrangement than any other. This arrangement is effective for a lecture; however, group interaction is difficult.

Classroom

In a classroom arrangement, the chairs face the front and tables provide a work surface for the audience. With this arrangement, the number of available seats is reduced about half compared to the auditorium or theater arrangement. Group interaction is also difficult, although one-way communication with the presenter is possible.

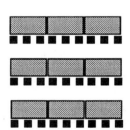

Modified Classroom

A modified classroom arrangement brings the audience closer to the front of the room and is arranged to focus attention more to the center of the stage area. This arrangement makes it easier for participants to see each other than in the regular classroom setup.

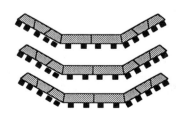

Trapezoid and rectangular tables are required if tables are to fit together.

V-Shape or Herringbone Pattern

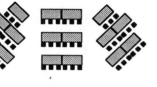

Another variation of the classroom arrangement that does not require trapezoid tables is a V-shape or a herringbone pattern. More floor space is required, but people can move more freely and have small group discussions easier. The herringbone pattern is similar to the V-shape, but with the center row omitted.

U-Shape

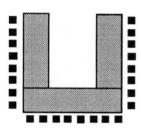

A U-shape arrangement allows for face-to-face participation and discussion. Fewer people can be seated, but the presenter can move into the center of the group if desired.

Circular

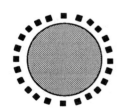

A circular arrangement can be made with or without tables. This arrangement is top-notch for creating an environment to foster total group interaction. However, the arrangement is difficult if you are going to use a projector and screen, since a number of the participants will have to reposition themselves to view the screen.

Cluster/Round Tables

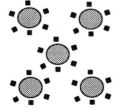

Cluster arrangements of four to six individuals may be formed with or without tables. This arrangement is excellent for small-group discussion and lots of interaction, but the focus on a speaker and the use of media are difficult.

Combination

These arrangements represent only the very basic options that are possible. You can combine them to come up with any number of other arrangements. You need to be careful, however, that an arrangement serves the number of people attending and is effective for the activities you have planned.

Seating Capacity Matrix*

Room Size	Auditorium Theater Seating Capacity 10 sq ft/person	Classroom Modified Seating Capacity 20 sq ft/person	Boardroom Rectangular Seating Capacity 30 sq ft/person	U-Shape Hollow Square Seating Capacity 40 sq ft/person
20' x 20'	40	20	13	10
20' x 40'	80	40	26	20
30' x 30'	90	45	30	22
30' x 40'	120	60	40	30
30' x 50'	150	75	50	37
40' x 40'	160	80	53	40
40' x 50'	200	100	66	50
50' x 50'	250	125	83	62

–Kory Terlaga
Training Room Solutions
Howe Furniture Corporation

* Note that the terms by Howe Furniture Corporation vary slightly from those used in this book.

Most hotels will have a similar type of seating plan.

Ergonomics of the Presentation

Ergonomics is a study of relationships between individuals and the environment. The ergonomic factors of your speaking environment can directly influence and contribute to the success of your presentation. Ergonomic factors to consider are: lighting, acoustics, climatization, color, and safety.

Lighting

Lighting is a major concern. Efficient lighting should illuminate the room while you are speaking, but you need to be able to adjust the lights if you are using media. Natural lighting should be controllable by blinds or blackout shades to darken the room for media presentations.

Lighting is classified as ambient, task, or accent. Ambient lighting refers to the general illumination in a room. Task lighting provides direct light to illuminate a visual task area, such as a light on the lectern so you can see your notes. Parabolic lighting with diffusers to direct light down is good for audience notetaking visibility, yet provides a soft overall light. Accent lighting, such as a spot light, provides directional lighting to focus on one area.

A footcandle (fc) is a unit of measurement used to determine light density. Reading and other detailed tasks require 70 to 100 fc. The viewing of a videotape should be approximately 60 to 70 fc for the audience; projected media of overhead transparencies and slides should be approximately 5 to 20 fc. Thus, with the proper lighting controls, you can accommodate two different activities, such as the notetaking and the viewing of the visuals.

Separate controls for lights throughout the room and dimmers are helpful devices in lighting the room properly for media presentations. An ideal situation is to be able to turn out the overhead lights completely, except for task lighting in the front of the room, and dim them in the middle and back sections of the room.

This arrangement allows enough light for the audience to take notes, to keep eye contact with the speaker, and to view the visuals. Darkening the area near the screen will give the visuals a higher contrast and more clarity. For instance, a visual with a blue background will show a faded blue with overhead light reflecting on the screen, but can become a vivid blue without the lights.

When presenting in an unfamiliar setting, be sure to survey the room before your presentation. Find the light switches and experiment with the lights to find the best combination(s) for maximum visibility. Hopefully, you can control the lights from the front of the room. If not, ask an audience member to help you as needed.

Acoustics

Noise irritates people and breaks their concentration. Unwanted sounds can travel through openings in walls, floors, ceilings, ventilating ducts, outlet boxes, and under or around doors. You may engage a room in a hotel that seems very quiet, but arrive for your presentation and find a motivational sales meeting in an adjacent room. The noise could be quite disruptive. Therefore, if possible, find out what types of meetings are scheduled near your room before choosing your location.

Architectural materials and interior design elements can effectively isolate or absorb unwanted noises. Carpets, drapes, and acoustical tiles all absorb sound; glass and smooth hard surfaces reflect sounds.

Sound intensity is measured in decibels (db). The human ear has a hearing range of decibels from 1 to 130 db. Because the decibel scale is logarithmic, what may seem like a small increase in decibels is actually a large increase in sound intensity. A rise of 10 decibels on the scale amounts to a doubling of the sound level. Comfortable sound levels in a presentation room should be about 50 to 60 db. Outside noises of more than 60 decibels will create a noisy environment in which an audience will have difficulty in listening. People can only effectively listen and concentrate on one thing at a time.

Decibel Levels	
20 dB	rustling leaves
30 dB	soft whisper
40 dB	library
50 dB	quiet office
70 dB	light traffic
80 dB	typical factory
90 dB	heavy city traffic
100 dB	symphony
110 dB	rock concert
120 dB	aircraft takeoff
140 dB	threshold of pain

Climate

An audience may suffer annoyance and dissatisfaction from the climate of the room and lose interest in your presentation without even realizing the problem is the climate and not your presentation. For instance, they may be drowsy and fall asleep from a room too warm—not from your speech.

Heating, ventilation, and air conditioning systems (HVAC) are combined to help control the interior climate for the comfort and well-being of the people in the room. The majority of people will prefer a temperature ranging from 70 to 72 degrees if they are passively sitting; however, if they become more actively involved in group work, they might prefer a temperature of 68 to 70 degrees. However, body size, age, activity level, and the closeness of the people to each other all affect the temperature.

Be careful in setting the temperature—some people may be burning up while others are freezing.

Humidity should be in the range of 40 to 60 percent. Ventilation, or air movement, is important to comfort, because lack of air exchange leads to stagnation and pollution. Air velocity of about 25 feet a minute is recommended. Legislation making smoking in public places illegal is helping to provide clean air in conference and meeting rooms.

Poor climate factors can impede your presentation, and good climate factors can enhance your presentation. Thus, you should be aware of these environmental factors. You may not always be able to control them effectively; but you will develop a better rapport with the audience if you are sensitive to the environment. If the room becomes too warm (and you have no control on the thermostat), perhaps you can open doors or windows or provide an extra break-time. Talk with the audience and let them know you are aware of the environmental problems.

Color and Decor

Color can create moods, influence physical comfort or discomfort, contribute to attitudes, influence behavior, and affect the perception of time and space. Colors used in the room environment can affect your audience. This is similar to the effects mentioned in Chapter 7 concerning the use of color in your visuals.

Popular, appropriate shades for the walls of a presentation room are pastel colors or soft earth tones. These colors are calming and not distracting. On the other hand, high-energy colors—such as bright red, yellow, blue, and orange—might be effective for an employee lounge or break room. The bright colors would create an atmosphere of high stimulation and promote enthusiasm among participants before they come back into the more calming presentation room.

The decor should be pleasant but not distracting. For instance, pictures, wall mountings, and other decorations can be so intriguing that they are distracting. Even a clock can be distracting. For that reason, many presentation rooms will place a clock at the back of the room, allowing the presenter to be aware of the time for proper pacing. Audience members can turn around and look at it on occasion but not become overly conscious of the time.

Safety

A last, but very important, consideration in the presentation environment is safety. In choosing your presentation room, you need to observe the location of the outlets and decide whether your cords and cables will be long enough. You may have to take an electrical extension cord and/or a long remote control for the slide projector with you. Extreme caution should be used with cords or cables to prevent stumbling by participants or even yourself. Use duct tape to secure cords close to the floor when they must cross an aisle.

Most rooms and facilities will have legal regulations stating the maximum number of people permitted in a room. Regulations may limit room arrangements. Emergency evacuation procedures may be provided or posted in the room. As a presenter, you may find yourself as the one in charge for an emergency evacuation. Therefore, it is important for you to be aware of the emergency procedures and closest exits.

Your visuals are ready! You have checked out the environment! What is next? Chapter 9 addresses the issue of becoming competent in presenting.

References

Minnesota Western Visual Presentation Systems Catalog. Oakland: San Francisco Bay Area, Northern California Corporate Headquarters, 160.

Terlaga, Kory. (1990). *Training Room Solutions.* Howe Furniture Corporation, 42.

An artist's drawing of a
model meeting room.
Courtesy of Minnesota
Western Visual
Presentation Systems.

An aesthetically designed boardroom showing the placement of an overhead projector and a video playback unit. Courtesy of California Portland Cement Company, Glendora, California.

This meeting room has an adjacent kitchen and pantry which are conveniently accessible through the opening of sliding doors. Courtesy of California Portland Cement Company, Glendora, California.

A training room using computer-generated visuals. The room seats 35 people comfortably in director-type chairs. Courtesy of Graphix Zone Resource Center, Irvine, California.

A modern training room called the Learning Center. Courtesy of Southern California Edison Technology Application Center, Irwindale, California.

A small meeting room at CH2M Hill, Irvine, California. Photo by Jim Kupsh.

A classroom in the Lumpkin College of Business at Eastern Illinois University, Charleston, Illinois, with a tiered arrangement. Photo by Beatty Photographic Services.

Being a First-Rate Presenter

Good visuals can give you more confidence! They serve as guideposts. They replace the need for notecards and cue cards. However, they do not replace YOU, the speaker. You are the main attraction, and the visuals supplement! Therefore, your behavior is important. Personality traits, voice, movement and position, appearance, personal organization, and audience interaction all contribute to your competence in presenting.

Revealing Personality Traits

Personality traits of a speaker become visibly apparent during a presentation. These traits are contagious. If you show enthusiasm, the audience is more likely to become enthusiastic. If you show a sense of humor, the audience will, also; if you portray flexibility, the audience is likely to follow suit.

Enthusiasm

As a speaker, you must believe in your topic and be committed to your purpose. The object of a speech is to communicate, and conviction on your part is essential. You need to communicate information to motivate or to persuade the audience in some way.

Many people fear public speaking. Individuals may be poorly organized, unprepared, and ineffective in their delivery techniques. The use of visuals helps a presenter to have confidence and to be more relaxed during a presentation because of the detailed planning and organization required. However, the presenter should be aware of many other presenting techniques, also.

Several examples illustrate the importance of a speaker projecting enthusiasm. If you are a sales manager speaking at an annual sales meeting, you had better show your enthusiasm for the sales representatives. You also need to show (not just say) your loyalty to the company, your beliefs in the product, and your zest for a coming successful sales year.

Instead of using a very matter-of-fact manner in demonstrating a new type of computer software to an audience, you can project your like (or possibly dislike) for the software as you explain the facts. You may think your bias or prejudice is showing. It is. After all, the reason you are the speaker is to inform, teach, motivate, sell, or persuade.

If you are teaching a history course, your purpose is to not only relate facts to the class but to instill an appreciation for events that happened in the past and how they can relate to the future. A few history teachers have even portrayed historical roles, such as George Washington or Paul Revere, by appearing in costume.

> If you are not enthusiastic, how can you expect your audience to be enthusiastic?

However, you need to plan your strategy carefully before your presentation to be sure your enthusiasm is sincere and presents the image you want.

Humor

Humor can be a powerful tool for gaining and keeping attention, motivating people, and relieving stress. Many speakers avoid humor, believing they want to show they are serious and sincere about their topic. They may be afraid to use humor for fear of offending the audience or for fear that no one will laugh. Humor does not necessarily mean making people laugh loudly or "roll in the aisles." It can be much more subtle.

> Humor is a serious communication tool. It can gain attention, create rapport, and make ideas more memorable. If used properly, the camaraderie developed with laughter and play can diffuse hostility, open doors to team building, manage stress, increase creativity and problem solving, and tap the motivation of audiences, clients, employees, family, and friends.
>
> –Jackie Miller, President
> J. Miller Consultants

Learning how and when to be humorous is an important presentation technique. Humor should be natural–not forced. Telling a joke for the sake of including a joke will not be effective. Instead, include humor for a specific purpose or to communicate your understanding of a problem.

Smiling is one method of showing a sense of humor. When you smile, you demonstrate a sense of ease and confidence. Your audience will also become more comfortable and show you more warmth.

Some speakers can successfully use themselves as the brunt of a joke. However, this technique may be hard for a novice who is already a bit insecure in facing the audience. Another technique that might be better for beginners is to show a bit of humor in the visuals–such as using symbols or cartoons. The audience must never be the brunt of a joke. Do not risk offending people.

Malcolm Kushner, in his book titled *The Light Touch: How to Use Humor for Business Success*, states the following reasons for including humor for business success.

✔ A study of 100 executives at America's largest corporations disclosed that 84 percent thought employees with a sense of humor do a better job than those with little or no sense of humor.

✔ A survey of 737 chief executives of large corporations found that 98 percent said they would hire a person with a good sense of humor over one who lacks humor.

✔ A well-known health letter recently reported that when humor is part of the work situation, both individual and group productivity often increase.

Use humor to make your ideas more memorable, to clarify points, to persuade or motivate your listeners. In turn, the audience will know you are a friendly and caring person.

Flexibility

Always plan for the unknown. The time allowed for your presentation may be shortened or lengthened. Your materials may not be available (take all precautions to see this does not happen, but . . .), or someone else on the program covered your subject before your presentation.

Since you cannot plan for all the possible things that could go wrong, be willing to roll with the punches. Remember to keep a sense of humor.

> If things go wrong, they will go wrong at the worst possible time.
>
> If everything is going okay, you have obviously overlooked something.
>
> Murphy's Laws

Maximizing Personal Appearance

The audience sees you before they hear you. They form an impression of you before you utter that first word. Therefore, both dress and posture are important issues in making a presentation.

Dress

Dress includes all personal grooming habits, such as neatness and cleanliness, as well as your clothes. You want to be comfortable but also appropriate for the occasion of your presentation.

Appropriateness for your presentation is important. You want to fit into a particular setting or environment. Close your eyes and mentally visualize a corporate business person, a physician, a musician, a construction worker, a clerical worker, a student, a child, an adult, etc. Then, decide what type of image you want to portray to your audience.

A speaker need not adjust to exactly what the audience is wearing but should be somewhat similar in most instances. Be careful to avoid being either too drab or too showy. If in doubt, however, it is usually better to be too formal rather than too informal.

> If in doubt, be conservative and dress in business attire rather than casual wear for your speaking engagement.

Posture

Stand in an erect position with both feet firmly planted on the floor (not together but about six or eight inches apart) and with your shoulders back. This posture conveys confidence and good self esteem. You will look like you want to be there. This body language will communicate to the audience even before you begin speaking.

Building Personal Organization

The audience will form an impression of you based on your personal organization habits. If you look like you have it together, the audience will consider you more credible and will become unconsciously more receptive.

Notes

Notes are permissible; however, good visuals can frequently replace the need for a lot of detailed notes, since the visuals serve as an outline for you as well as for the audience. In a sense, the visuals will serve as memory joggers for you.

You also may need to have a few facts or figures as notes. The notes feature included in most presentation software provides an excellent method of having speaker notes. The visual is shown at the top with a half page left for notes, which can be keyed in large, bold type. Before printing, number the pages in case they should get out of order.

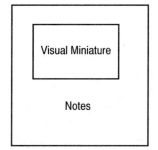

However you prepare your notes, make them easy to use and easy to read. Remember to avoid all capital letters. If you decide to use cards, select the larger 4- x 6-inch or 5- x 8-inch size. The smaller 3- x 5-inch cards do not hold enough information and will require too much switching. You do not need extra opportunities to show nervousness.

Materials

Organize props or other materials that you use so they are in order and readily available when and as you need them. An audience should not have to wait on you to shuffle through your materials to find the right prop.

Equipment

Your equipment should be set up and ready to go before the presentation. You are the responsible person for seeing that everything is set up and in working condition before your presentation begins. Additional information on this subject is given in Chapter 11.

Controlling Vocal Elements

Your voice and your visuals deliver the message to the audience. Voice plays a major role in both getting and retaining audience interest.

Articulation and Enunciation

Articulation involves speaking distinctly and clearly. For good enunciation, avoid slurring words together or cutting off the ends of the words.

Modulation and Pitch

Modulating or changing the pitch of your voice can add variation and provide interest in your speaking. Avoid speaking in a monotone voice that may be pleasant but will put the audience to sleep.

Volume, Emphasis, and Pace

Sufficient volume is important. If an audience has to strain to hear you, they may unconsciously decide to just tune you out and daydream. If a microphone is provided, you probably need to make use of it.

Microphones (mikes) come in three different forms. One is a *stationary mike* that lets you keep your hands free but holds you to one spot. A *lavaliere-type mike* can be clipped to your clothing and usually comes with a long cord which will allow you to walk around a bit. *Cordless microphones* allow you to walk around without getting tangled in the long cord.

Visit the room before your presentation to practice and get comfortable with a microphone. Be sure a stationary mike is adjusted to the right height for you–usually about chin height and six inches away. Avoid blowing into a mike, but speak into it to be sure the volume is at the right level.

Variations in volume, emphasis, and pace are effective in gaining and keeping interest. Make sure a variation or change is used at the proper time. For instance, you may want to increase your volume and emphasis on an important point. Or, you may want to pause a bit after a thought-provoking statement or idea to allow time for the audience to absorb the idea. Variations of some type serve as punctuation before going into a different point or before starting your ending summary.

Utilizing Position and Movement

In addition to your appearance and your voice, you need to consider position and movement. These factors can either contribute to the presentation effectiveness or be a distraction.

Location

The location of where you stand to speak is important. Usually, facilities will have a lectern or specified place established in the front of the room. Check to be sure this position does not block your visuals.

Think about positioning at the front of the room from the audience's viewpoint. Many authorities believe the best location for a speaker is to the right side (if you are facing the audience) of where the visuals will be projected. The audience will focus on the speaker before their eyes move on to the visuals. This arrangement capitalizes on the natural reading movement from left to right.

> Some experts believe that you should locate yourself on the right side of the screen (as you face the audience). This placement makes it natural for the audience to look at you and then the visual.

Eye Contact

Making eye contact with members of the audience is extremely important in establishing rapport. Even before you say one word, take time to look at the audience, from one side of the room to the other. People like to be noticed, and this moment of eye contact helps to signal that you are relaxed and ready to speak to them.

Maintain eye contact with members of the audience throughout the presentation. Some speakers find it helpful to pick out a few friendly faces and focus eye contact with them to be inspired by their enthusiasm. However, you should be careful to maintain eye contact throughout the audience. Make each member of the audience think that you are making contact. Do not look over the heads of the audience, look at one side of the room only, or scan the audience so fast that you never really make eye contact with anyone. If you are especially shy, you might try looking at eyebrows instead of eyes until you gain confidence.

Gestures and Mannerisms

Gestures and mannerisms should be natural. Avoid a robotic military stance but do not become too casual or relaxed. Be careful that you do not grab hold of a lectern or microphone and appear to be holding on for dear life. Also avoid nervously clutching notecards, pens, or other objects.

Hands can and should make natural gestures similar to what you might do in talking to an individual on a one-to-one basis. Gestures can be used to emphasize points. You may want to use a pointer to illustrate points on your visual.

Practice gestures in front of a mirror. An even better technique is to videotape a portion of your entire presentation. Then watch it by turning the sound down and evaluating your gestures as well as your mannerisms to see what looks effective and what is distracting.

Body Language or Nonverbal Communications

Body language or nonverbal communications can express a lot about you to the audience. The following list illustrates a few of the signals you may be sending. These same types of nonverbal communications may help you read members of your audience.

- ✔ *Insecure and Nervous*—constant jerking movements of the entire body or hands, playing with objects, maintaining poor eye contact. These same traits portrayed by audience members may mean boredom, also.
- ✔ *Defensive*—crossing arms in front, making a fist, or pointing a finger.
- ✔ *Cooperative*—opening hands, looking alert, tilting head, holding upper body forward.
- ✔ *Thinking*—using hand-to-face gestures, scratching head, stroking chin, removing glasses.

Encouraging Interaction

Most audiences like to become involved in some way in the presentation. Involvement does not require giving members of the audience a chance to speak, but can be as subtle as asking for a show of hands on various issues.

Audience Participation

Audience participation makes an audience become

involved. At the beginning of a presentation, for example, you can make use of a show of hands to determine demographic information. This technique provides you with key information about your group and also gives them information about each other. You may have other activities they can do as audience members. Perhaps you need assistance of some type, or you may want to ask a few key questions to elicit individual responses.

Actually, you can involve your audience by stimulating their minds into visualizing various situations—such as asking people to close their eyes and visualize how they would feel if they walked into their office and saw the desk clear of paperwork, or if they found a new computer, etc.

Questions and Answers

Many times it may be appropriate to allow time for a question-and-answer period at the end of your presentation. If you do not know an answer, be willing to admit that. Ask if anyone in the audience can answer. If this technique does not provide an answer, you could offer to find out and get back to the individual.

Asking people to leave their business cards, with a note for follow-up information or additional questions, is also a good technique to use. Be sure to follow up, however, once you have promised.

A large number of questions is a signal that you need to analyze your materials and make adjustments before using them again. You may have motivated people into being really interested and involved in your topic; or, you did not cover the topic adequately.

A lack of questions may mean either that you covered the topic adequately or that you bored the audience until no one really cares. You decide which is the case!

Additional ideas for evaluating your presentation are discussed in Chapter 11. However, sometimes you may be conducting a meeting rather than making a presentation. This topic is discussed in Chapter 10.

References

Kushner, Malcolm. (1990). *The Light Touch: How to Use Humor for Business Success.* New York: Simon and Schuster, 21-22.

Miller, Jackie. (President, J. Miller Consultants, Human Resource Development and Education). Printed in *Minnesota Western Visual Presentation Systems Catalog.*

Conducting Meetings

This chapter contains information helpful in case you find you are in charge of conducting a meeting. The success of the individual speakers or presenters can depend upon the success of you as the leader.

Effective meeting management is an increasingly important topic for today's businesses, governments, and a variety of other organizations. Good meetings are essential to overall organizational productivity," explains Virginia Johnson, manager of the 3M Meeting Management Institute. "With corporations constantly restructuring and competitive pressures mounting, it is essential for businesspeople to communicate important ideas, plans, and concerns within their organizations. The forum for this type of activity is meetings, of course. But meetings need to be effectively planned and directed—just like any other business component—in order to be productive.

Meeting Management News
Volume 1, Number 1
3M Meeting Management Institute

M eetings are necessary! But are they effective? The Annenberg School of Communications at the University of Southern California conducted a report of 903 people from 36 small, medium, and large companies in both the public and private sectors to find out information about meetings. Their findings indicate the following profile of a typical meeting in corporate America:

✔ begins at 11 A.M.

✔ is called with two hours notice–if not regularly scheduled

✔ is attended by nine people–usually two managers, four co-workers, two subordinates, and one outsider

✔ is a staff meeting (44 percent), with others being task force (23 percent) and information sharing (20 percent)

The same survey indicates that satisfaction with the meeting is correlated with:

✔ job satisfaction

✔ meeting leaders

✔ attendees

✔ agenda and the extent to which it is covered

✔ decision of meeting outcome

✔ amount of individual participation in the meeting

✔ amount of preparation

✔ presentation effectiveness

✔ amount of time spent talking about irrelevant issues

> *A Profile of Meetings in Corporate America:*
> *Results of the 3M Meeting Effectiveness Study*

Cost and Productivity

Minnesota Western Visual Presentation Systems is a company specializing in products for meetings and presentations. Its general rule for estimating the cost of a meeting is to double the hourly base pay of all participants for each hour met. Doubling the cost of each person's salary allows for other expenses such as payroll taxes, benefits, general overhead, meeting preparation, travel time, visual aids, and visual-aid equipment.

According to the dictionary, a meeting is the act or process of coming together for a business, social, or religious purpose, yet few people know how to properly attend, organize, or conduct a meeting. Dave Barry (September, 1986) compares the modern business meeting with a funeral: "You have a gathering of people who are wearing uncomfortable clothing and would rather be somewhere else. The major difference is that most funerals have a definite purpose. Also, nothing is ever really buried in a meeting."

Hourly Cost of Meetings
Number of Attendees

Annual Salary	2	4	6	8	10	20
$62,500	$125	$250	$375	$500	$625	$1,250
$50,000	100	200	300	400	500	1,000
$37,500	75	150	225	300	375	750
$25,000	50	100	150	200	250	500
$12,500	25	50	75	100	125	250

Minnesota Western Visual Presentation Systems

Reasons Not *to Meet*

Many times you should not call a meeting. You may find that a memo, phone call, or electronic message between computers would accomplish the same information-sharing objectives easier and with less expense. You, as well as members within the group, may not have done enough homework and should wait to gather additional information before meeting as a group. If you have already made a decision, do not call a meeting to discuss alternatives unless you are open to changing your mind.

When members of a group are upset or hostile, do not call a meeting unless you want to be hung or burned at the stake. Instead, meet individually with members of the group. Also, one-on-one meetings are necessary whenever you are dealing with issues such as hiring, firing, and other personal problems.

Reasons to Meet

A group meeting should be scheduled when you have information or concerns that would most effectively be shared by the group as a whole. While announcements can be shared in a newsletter, memo, or electronic message, you may need to emphasize or personally call attention to certain issues.

Group training methods can be effective in many situations. For instance, if you need to provide instructions for new equipment, you may find it far more productive to have a group training session versus furnishing an instructor for one-on-one training. Individual training would not be cost efficient.

Meetings are necessary for problem solving and/or decision making. You, as a leader of the meeting, have an important role in seeing that the meeting is effective. Conducting an effective meeting requires guidelines in preparation for before, during, and after the meeting, similar to the planning steps given in Chapters 2 and 9 for planning your individual presentation. However, some specific guidelines for meetings are given next.

Before the Meeting

Once the location is determined, preparation before a meeting consists of notification, objectives, agenda, ground rules, and research. These topics are essential if you are to have a successful and productive meeting.

Notification

The amount of notification given to members expected to attend a meeting will vary based on the circumstance. Meetings requiring participants to travel

> One of the reasons a meeting may be ineffective is that the right people are not present.

some distance should be scheduled several weeks or even months ahead of time. This allows individuals to make travel plans and arrange to get away from their offices.

Even meetings held by a company within a single facility, however, require advance notification to allow the attendees to schedule other appointments and activities. Of course, emergency meetings may be needed that prevent this advance notice, but be careful the emergency is not because of your oversight in scheduling.

Reminders, either by mail or phone, are helpful—particularly for meetings scheduled long in advance. After all, participants must be there to have an effective meeting.

Objectives

Every meeting should have specific objectives for what is to be accomplished during the meeting. These objectives should be communicated to participants before the meeting so they have a chance to think about what is to be accomplished. They also can prepare to bring any materials that might be needed.

Agenda

Every meeting should have an agenda to support the objective(s). Make it easy to read, action-oriented, time-sequenced, and show who is responsible for what.

One way of communicating your objectives is with an agenda. An agenda should include all pertinent information about beginning and ending times, dates, place, topics, and responsibilities. Write the agenda in a positive tone that gives the idea of opportunities rather than problems. The agenda sent a day or two before the meeting can serve as a reminder.

In general, agendas also should include the objective(s), a time list for individual discussion items, and action-oriented tasks to be accomplished. A list of who is responsible for what topic in the meeting might also be a good inclusion so people can be prepared.

Creating an agenda also makes you plan better. You must order items logically, then estimate time lines to see if you can cover all the items listed in your objectives.

Even though you send agendas out before the meeting, do not expect everyone to arrive with their copy. Make additional copies for distribution at the meeting.

Product Management Meeting

Agenda

November 12, 1995
10:30–12:15

Objective:	To identify, evaluate, and prioritize new applications for Widget X
10:30–10:45	• Review list of current applications *—Wagner*
10:45–11:15	• Create list of new applications *—All*
11:15–11:30	• Break
11:30–11:45	• Prioritize best recommendations *—Johnson*
11:45–12:05	• Action plan and assignments *—Smith*
12:05–12:15	• Wrap-up and feedback *—Wagner*

—Minnesota Western Visual Presentation Systems

Ground Rules

As a leader, you need to set the ground rules on the style and tone of the meeting. Meetings should start on time and stick to the agenda. If a meeting is scheduled for 3:00 P.M., you should start it promptly at 3:00. One school of thought is that, perhaps, you should not schedule a meeting on the hour or even half hour but at 3:09 or 4:36 P.M., stressing the idea to individuals that promptness is desired. If you get in the habit of always starting a meeting late, people will automatically start arriving late. The "early birds" may easily become disturbed and lose their prompt habits.

Determine the formality, style, and tone that best fits your situation. Remember–if the meeting fails, the blame will fall on you. If the meeting is successful, you have an outstanding group of people; however, you also will receive recognition for a job well done.

Research

Are you prepared for the meeting? Research preparation consists of locating any needed information or tools. You are responsible for either obtaining the proper background materials or delegating the task to someone else.

During the Meeting

As a leader of the meeting, you are the commanding officer in charge. Whatever does or does not happen is a direct reflection on you.

Organization

The objectives and agenda should help you keep organized, but they do not do the task alone. You must see to it that your plan of action is followed appropriately. The time of the meeting participants costs your company money; as meeting leader, you are the person held accountable.

Time Schedule

Interruptions may happen, but try to stick to the time schedule you set. Make the participants aware of your goal of adhering to the time schedule on the agenda. They will appreciate your concern for their time.

Be sure your speakers or presenters stick to their time schedules. If you ask for a 20-minute presentation, be sure to allow that amount of time.

If you follow the time schedule on the agenda, you can have either presenters or attendees arrive and leave accordingly. It may not be necessary to have all people in attendance throughout the meeting. This approach to meetings can help participants handle other pressing needs and still be available as needed for the meeting. It also demonstrates the necessity of adhering to a predetermined schedule.

Introductions

Introductions of speakers or presenters at the meeting are important unless the speaker is a member of the group. Even then, some background information of why that person is an expert or has been chosen is helpful.

If the speaker is not a member of the group, contact that person to get some background information, a bibliography sheet, or a vitae before the meeting. Receiving this information before the meeting will give you time to prepare a brief, positive introduction of the presenter.

In introducing a speaker or presenter, you have the responsibility of setting the tone and the mood. Make the audience eager to hear the speaker. Your enthusiasm, or lack of it, will be contagious. Highlight the presenter's background and give a few supporting bits of information to show why the person is an authority on the presentation to be given. Keep the introduction brief; do not take up too much of the speaker's time.

Reactions

> After introducing a speaker, listen attentively. The audience may be watching you.

After a presentation is finished, thank the speaker publicly. Reacting to specific points or statements shows involvement and appreciation. In a sense, you are the cheerleader for the audience. At conferences or conventions, many organizations will provide outside presenters with a token gift in appreciation of their contribution.

Participation/Interaction

> As appropriate, encourage participation and interaction from the audience. People like to become involved.

Participation and interaction are the keys to successful meetings and conferences. People like to become involved. If they are only passive listeners, you might as well have made a recording and sent it to them. Keep in mind the reason for a meeting is to share and discuss information—not just receive.

If your time schedule does not allow for discussion, you may want to ask the speaker to be available after the session or during a break for individual discussion—if this arrangement is possible.

Questions/Answers

Allow time for a question-and-answer period in either a presentation or a general meeting. You, as either the leader or the speaker, should always repeat the question before answering. The reason is simple. People in the back of the room may not be able to hear a question asked in the front of the room, and vice versa. Hearing an answer to a question without knowing the question is confusing and frustrating.

Ending

At the end of a meeting, a synopsis or brief summary of the accomplishments is important. You want people to leave on a high note, feeling their time was well spent. Usually, the last announcement at a meeting should be concerning the next meeting–mention of when, where, and what. You may also want to thank members for their attendance and participation.

After the Meeting

Responsibilities do not end when the meeting adjourns. In addition to returning the room to its original condition, you still have several responsibilities and duties to accomplish as a leader.

Summaries or Minutes

Written summaries or minutes of a meeting are valuable for several reasons. First, you may need written documentation of the decisions, accomplishments, etc. In many situations, it is helpful to distribute this information to members who attended. It is also important for distribution to individuals not in attendance at the meeting.

Distribute the summaries or minutes promptly. With the technology available today, it is possible to hand participants this information at the end of the meeting. The equipment necessary may not be feasible for you, or you may want to take a little more time in preparing the materials before distribution. In any event, the materials should be distributed in a timely manner–usually within a day or two after the meeting.

> What did we do?

Activities

Having a meeting and deciding to do activities does not automatically mean the tasks will be done. During the meeting, assignments should be designated–for you, members of the group, or others. As a leader, you have the responsibility of seeing that the activities are carried out. Distribution of the written summary or minutes is one way of reminding members of what needs to be done.

> Who is to do what?

Evaluation

After a meeting, you need to evaluate the quality of your meeting. You need to ask yourself the following questions:

> How did we do?

✔ Were the meeting objectives met?

✔ Did we follow the time schedule?

✔ Did we complete the agenda?

✔ Did attendees participate?

✔ Did the right people attend?

✔ Did they arrive on time?

✔ Were future assignments or tasks clearly made?

✔ Were decisions made?

✔ Was the meeting productive?

✔ Were plans clearly made?

✔ What was the general reaction of the participants after the meeting?

✔ What improvements can we make for the next meeting to make it better?

Electronic Meetings

Electronic meetings are not a wave of the future but are taking place today. Actually, an electronic meeting can take on many different meanings and variations. Electronic technology is used in preparing and projecting visuals and in preparing handouts, agendas, minutes, notetaking, etc.   People may be notified of meetings either by electronic or voice mail. Minutes or notes of the meeting can be distributed at the end of the meeting by using an electronic copyboard.

However, many meetings are becoming even more electronic within the meeting room. A computer connected to the company network can be a real asset for a meeting. For instance, if information is needed from the database, it is immediately accessible.

General classifications of electronic meetings are telephone, video, computer conferences, and group-decision support systems.

Telephone Conference

A teleconference allows numerous people from various locations to speak with one another using the

telephones, without physically traveling to one location. This type of electronic meeting has been used effectively for many years.

Video Conference

A video conference provides video as well as audio for the conference–commonly referred to as video-conferencing. Videoconferencing has been available for several years. A drawback has been the necessity of having participants assemble in either a public or private studio. Nonetheless, videoconferencing is being used successfully for many different types of meetings or conferences throughout the world. Even though the rental of a videoconference facility may be expensive, the meeting is usually considerably less expensive than the combined travel cost of the participants.

Computer Conference

Computer conferences allow individuals to communicate from their own computers to other individuals at their computers via a modem and telephone lines. A computer conference can range from within a single room or company location to locations throughout the world.

Participants in a computer conference key in their remarks that are transmitted to the screens of the other participants. A participant can key back an answer–thus, the meeting becomes very similar to one in which individuals interact in person.

Computer conferencing can be active with all participants online. Or, the information can be stored until the participant comes online and asks for messages–such as electronic mail.

Group-Decision Support Systems

Group-decision support systems get participants involved by using either a keypad or a typewriter-like keyboard. For example, after discussion, a leader could transmit one or more questions to all the computers in the system. Questions can be arranged in multiple choice, true/false, or other formats.

Participants answer the questions and then return their responses to the host computer where their votes are recorded. The computer will then process the responses and display them in a matrix or graphic form. This can be displayed on an overhead projector with a projection panel. The information can then be discussed as well as stored on disk for referral later or for printed reports.

Keyboard systems which allow participants to type words or narrative rather than just numbers are also available. Therefore, the leader can ask open-ended questions and get results from participants to be viewed by the audience members as well as stored on a disk for future use.

Computer meetings can have a real role for sensitive subjects. Many diverse opinions can be gathered because participants respond actively but remain anonymous. The entire process can remain highly confidential. However, the person controlling the host computer can tell which computer the input came from. Also, a person can type a name after an entry to let others know who contributed the idea. As with any new technology, ground rules and leadership are needed.

> Group-decision support systems are useful tools in conducting effective meetings.

Meetings, similar to presentations, require a careful look at delivery techniques. In addition, a meeting should be evaluated to measure its effectiveness and determine how the next meeting can be made better. These topics are the subject of Chapter 11.

References

Barry, Dave. (September, 1986). "How to Attend a Meeting." *Reader's Digest*, 136-138.

Monge, Peter; McSween, Charles; and Wyer, JoAnne. (November, 1989). *A Profile of Meeting in Corporate America: Results of the 3M Meeting Effectiveness Study.* Los Angeles: Annenberg School of Communications, University of Southern California.

Meeting Management News, Volume 1, Number 1. Austin, Texas: 3M Meeting Management Institute, 3M Center.

Delivering and Evaluating

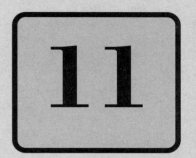

P lanning, preparing, and developing speech competence are all vital elements of a presentation. The final step consists of delivering the presentation and evaluating the presentation after it has been delivered.

Delivering and evaluating a presentation can be divided into "before," "during," and "after." This chapter discusses necessary ingredients and activities during each of these three stages and how they can make a presentation effective.

Before the Presentation

Before a presentation, secure or engage the needed materials and equipment. Give attention to the room itself. Preview, rehearse, and review many times. Prepare yourself–both physically and mentally. Be sure to take care of your personal physical needs–such as getting a good night's sleep and eating properly. Finally, make sure you arrive on time with all your materials.

Materials/Equipment

Professional overhead transparencies or 35 mm slides will be useless for your presentation if you are lacking the proper equipment on which to project them to your audience. The following section will give you general ideas of questions to ask yourself before the presentation concerning media you select to use.

Models/Replicas.
✔ Do you have all the models, replicas, or props called for in your speech?

✔ Are they complete?

✔ Will a table or stand be needed for the model?

✔ Is one model/replica enough, or should you have more?

Handouts.

✔ Do you have enough (better too many than not enough) handouts for the anticipated audience size?

✔ Are the handouts collated and packaged (stapled into packets or placed in folders) so they can be distributed quickly?

✔ Have you determined when and how you are going to hand them out?

✔ Do your speaker notes include when each handout will be mentioned or explained?

Posters and Flip Charts.

✔ Where are you going to display the posters or flip charts?

✔ Do you need a stand?

✔ Is masking tape needed?

✔ Are marking pens needed?

✔ What about push pins?

Notetakers/Copyboards.

✔ Do you have the right marking tools to use on the copyboard?

✔ Is there enough paper for your needs?

✔ Is the notetaker/copyboard working properly?

Overhead Transparencies.

✔ Are the overhead transparencies framed properly?

✔ Is the equipment placed in the best position for audience viewing?

✔ Is the projected image large enough?

✔ Do you have extra transparencies or marking pens in case you want to make last-minute or on-the-spot visuals?

✔ Does the overhead projector work?

✔ Do you know how to change the focus if needed?

✔ If the bulb in the overhead projector should burn out, where is another one?

✔ Do you know how to replace it?

✔ If needed, do you have a pointer?

35 mm Slides.

✔ Are the slides placed in the tray so they project properly?

✔ Are they in the proper order?

✔ Did you include a blank, black slide wherever you need to pause to address a topic not included in your slides?

✔ Is the remote control wireless or is the cord long enough to allow you to stand where you want or to walk around during the presentation?

✔ Are the cords placed so no one will stumble on them?

✔ Does the projector work?

✔ Is there an extra bulb?

✔ Do you know how to change it?

✔ Is the projector placed so the image is large enough to fill the screen?

✔ Do you know how to focus for a clearer picture?

✔ Do you know what to do in case a slide gets stuck?

✔ Do you need a pointer?

Computer-Based Media.

✔ Do you have the needed hardware and software, and does it work?

✔ Are the screen(s) adequate for audience viewing and placed in the most appropriate location?

✔ Do you know how to operate the equipment?

Room Arrangement

The overall presentation environment was discussed in Chapter 8. You may not be able to control environmental features, such as room arrangement, if you are part of an ongoing program. However, you need to be particularly alert to a few key items.

Find the light switch so you can adjust the lights for your needs. Look for a dimmer or see if there are separate controls allowing the front lights to be turned off and the back lights to remain on. You also need to check the microphone to see if it is working properly. If there will be a break, you should find out where the restrooms, water fountain, and refreshments are located.

Even when someone else is in charge and you are the guest speaker, you need to be aware of these factors. They can make a big difference in the final quality of your presentation.

> Where are the light switches?

Physical/Mental Self

Being ready for a presentation involves not only the tangibles of your materials, the equipment, and the room, but also your physical and mental self. Try to have your presentation ready several days before it is to be delivered, so you can relax and follow good health practices.

Observing health principles of nutrition, exercise, and rest are important. Staying up late and partying the night before a big presentation is taboo. Skipping breakfast to rehearse is also a poor idea.

If you are speaking as a part of a conference or convention program, you should, if possible, attend other presentations being given before yours. By observing others, you can pick up valuable information about topics being presented, general styles of presentation, attitude of the audience, and an overall feeling for the flavor of the conference.

These observations can have several general effects on you that can be quite positive. You can relate or tie your presentation into former comments or statements that have been made. If you are repeating something covered earlier, you can acknowledge that fact and make a case for the importance of the topic. In general, if other presentations are good, you will be challenged to keep up. If they are lousy, you will gain confidence that you have a real contribution to offer the group.

Preview, Rehearse, Review

Preview, rehearse, and review may seem like redundant words to you; but, the words accent the need to know what you are doing. You need to be familiar with your own materials as well as the presentation environment, including the equipment, room, and surroundings.

Previewing refers to checking that slides or other materials are arranged in the proper order. Rehearsing is actually going through the materials and giving the presentation. You may perform this step in an empty room or in front of one or more colleagues who can give you feedback. Reviewing is a process of going over your notes to refresh yourself on pertinent facts or figures that are to be included.

In general, these steps should be performed well before the presentation. Perhaps a last review is appropriate on the morning of the presentation, but do not put these steps off until presentation day. Be ready to relax and enjoy other activities, and you will be more refreshed to begin your own presentation.

During the Presentation

General principles to be followed were explained in Chapter 9. However, a few main points need to be re-emphasized, and procedures for obtaining evaluation feedback need to be discussed.

Audience Rapport

Developing a rapport with the audience is essential. If you have not been introduced–either by written information in the program or by an oral introduction–you may need to establish your credentials for speaking on the subject. Be factual but remain humble. Be one of the members of the audience; or, phrased another way, do not talk down to the group.

Try to get some feedback from the audience to give an indication of how you are doing. You might ask for participation in some way–ask for answers to your questions by a show of hands or by individual comments. Your audience rapport is also developed by personal eye contact with members of the audience.

Proper Media Principles

Proper media principles have been discussed throughout the book, but a few main points need reinforcement. They are extremely important in the overall effectiveness of your presentation.

- ✔ Turn a slide or overhead projector off whenever it is not being used for any length of time. The glaring light is distracting.

- ✔ Say more than the visuals say. Information on the visual is abbreviated; you are there to explain it more thoroughly.

> Media used improperly can be distracting and less effective than having no media.

✔ Address only the topic being shown on the visual while the visual is projected. If you wish to include comments on another subject when using slides, insert a template slide with nothing on it or a black slide. If using an overhead projector, you can either turn the projector off or place a blank piece of paper or file folder on the projection panel to prevent the glaring light on the screen.

✔ Frame overhead transparencies for ease of use and prevention of glare around the edges.

✔ Quickly slide the new transparency on the panel as you remove the old in order to prevent glare. Some people prefer to turn the projector on and off and then change the transparency. However, if you are using a number of transparencies, the click of the projector, as well as the extra time required, can become distracting.

✔ Focus people's attention on the point you are making by using a pointer or a buildup sequence.

✔ Stand in a position that does not block the screen.

✔ Remember that visuals are only an aid; you should be the center of attention.

Enthusiastic Attitude

If you are not enthusiastic and interested in your presentation, why should members of the audience be? Enthusiasm does not mean laughing, smiling, or being giddy, but does mean being genuinely interested. Remember—enthusiasm is contagious!

Evaluation Feedback

Evaluation feedback is important in finding out how you did and in determining strengths and weaknesses for future presentations. This feedback can be obtained in many ways.

First, you can observe the reactions and responses of the audience. However, keep in mind that some audiences may be warm and receptive, and others may be more formal and stiff. Geographic locations of where the people are from may affect their behavioral patterns and responses. For instance, one culture may smile and nod a lot; another may be extra warm and receptive; still another may be more stiff and formal. Yet, you may have given the very same presentation.

The occupation, type of group, or subject matter may contribute to the reaction of the audience. Even the time of day may make a difference. People usually are more quiet and reserved in the morning but become much more outgoing after lunch or before cocktail hour.

Being around after the presentation can be helpful. People will have the opportunity of talking with you on a one-to-one basis. From these conversations, you may receive important comments or feedback.

A more formal method of obtaining feedback is by using an evaluation form of some type. These forms can be simple and should be designed for quick completion by members of the audience. Design your evaluation form to give the type of information that will be valuable to you. A detailed presentation checklist and evaluation form for evaluating presentations is included at the end of this chapter, but you may want to design your own short one including three or four key questions. Make the form so that people can respond quickly and easily at the end of your presentation. Words such as "outstanding," "good," "okay," and "needs improvement" can be used. Or, you can use a 1 to 5 numbering scale; be sure you label clearly whether 1 is high or low.

Evaluation for _____

Directions: Circle the appropriate number and make any comments on the back of this sheet.

	High			*Low*	
Content	1	2	3	4	5
Delivery	1	2	3	4	5
Value	1	2	3	4	5

After the Presentation

Your presentation is not over when it is over! You still have some tasks at hand.

Cleanup

If you borrowed equipment or made room changes, be sure you return everything to its proper place after your presentation. Also, remember to pick up all your materials as you may want them again.

Self Examination

At some point before the day is over, stop and examine your own thoughts about the presentation.

✔ What do you think you did that was good?

✔ How can you improve this presentation or others in the future?

✔ What needs to be done that you did not do?

Make notes on these issues. If you wait until your next presentation, you may forget these observations and feelings if you have not jotted them down.

Participant Evaluation

Feedback from the audience is also important. The following items suggest ways to obtain feedback from your audience.

✔ Listen to the reactions from the audience.

✔ Were these the reactions you wanted?

✔ Study the evaluation forms.

✔ What are they really trying to tell you?

✔ Read between the lines.

Again, make notes and save them for when you are preparing your next presentation. These notes will refresh you on how you can improve.

Colleague Comments

Ask for feedback from close friends or colleagues who may have been in attendance. Analyze their reactions. Sometimes your best friends will not tell you negative comments, but give them a chance to give you feedback.

Revisions

Now, we can go back to the drawing board! With the ideas accumulated from your own feelings, verbal and written reactions from the audience participants, and reactions of colleagues–revise.

In the revision process, think of it as not only this particular presentation, in case you may be giving it again, but also of other presentations you may be making in the future. One general reaction many people have is to wish they had started and completed their preparation earlier. If this is the case, remember this fact and do so next time.

Keep in mind that no matter how great you were, you still need to concentrate on how to improve or what changes to make for the next time. You may want to examine other subjects or topics for future presentations. Just because you were good does not mean you should make a lifetime career out of that one presentation or those presentation techniques. Reach out and expand into new horizons for a next time!

One of the new horizons may be getting involved in multimedia presentations–the subject of the next chapter.

A method of improving your presentations is to observe and evaluate others. The following checklists and evaluation form can be duplicated and used in evaluating presentations. Note that the media/visuals category is given double points. The authors believe that this category is extremely important; however, you may change the emphasis and the points on the 50-point evaluation if you desire.

Presentation Checklist

and

Presentation Evaluation

Total Points _____ (50)

Content

Yes **No** 1. Was everything the speaker said technically correct?

Yes **No** 2. Did speaker include a sufficient amount of important points and relevant information?

Yes **No** 3. Was the material presented at a level of detail suitable to the intended audience?

Yes **No** 4. Has the speaker presented all the material clearly enough?

Yes **No** 5. Were the major points of the presentation fully explained and completely supported?

Yes **No** 6. Did illustrations and all other charts clearly relate to the discussion?

Yes **No** 7. Did the speaker cover about the right amount of material?

Yes **No** 8. Did the speaker seem to have an adequate knowledge of the subject?

List any comments you observed on the content of the presentation.

Organization

Yes   **No**   9.   Did the introduction give enough background information and prepare the audience?

Yes   **No**   10.   Was the purpose of the discussion clearly stated early in the presentation?

Yes   **No**   11.   Was the organization of the presentation obvious?

Yes   **No**   12.   Did the speaker's words and visuals give you sufficient clues about the organization?

Yes   **No**   13.   Did the speaker keep your attention throughout the presentation?

Yes   **No**   14.   Did the speaker move clearly/smoothly from point to point?

Yes   **No**   15.   Did the organization of the material seem logical to you?

Yes   **No**   16.   Was the conclusion clearly related to the main body of the discussion?

Yes   **No**   17.   Were the conclusions clearly presented?

List any comments you observed on the organization of the presentation.

Media/Visuals

Yes No   18.   Were the media/visuals appropriate for the subject?

Yes No   19.   Was there a sufficient number of visuals?

Yes No   20.   Were the visuals well designed?

Yes No   21.   Was today's technology for making visuals utilized properly?

Yes No   22.   Did the visuals add to the presentation?

Yes No   23.   Was the AV equipment set up and used appropriately?

Yes No   24.   Were handouts appropriate for the presentation?

Yes No   25.   Were handouts helpful/valuable?

Yes No   26.   Were handouts attractively designed?

Yes No   27.   Did the speaker tie in all the handouts/visuals/media with the talk?

List any comments you observed on the media/visuals used in the presentation.

Delivery

Yes　**No**　28.　Did the speaker appear relaxed, assured, and in command of the subject?

Yes　**No**　29.　Did the speaker move and gesture naturally?

Yes　**No**　30.　If the speaker used notes, were they handled in a way that was not distracting?

Yes　**No**　31.　Was the use of media distracting to the presentation in any way—such as overhead projector light left on without a visual.

Yes　**No**　32.　Did the speaker's posture appear to be natural and not distracting?

Yes　**No**　33.　Did the speaker project his/her voice sufficiently?

Yes　**No**　34.　Did the speaker speak at the right pace?

Yes　**No**　35.　Did the speaker make good eye contact with the audience?

Yes　**No**　36.　Was the speaker dressed appropriately for the intended audience and the purpose?

List any comments you observed on the delivery of the presentation.

Presentation Evaluation

Content
_____ **Points**

1   2   3   4   5   6   7   8   9   10
Awful   Poor   Average   Good   Outstanding

Organization
_____ **Points**

1   2   3   4   5   6   7   8   9   10
Awful   Poor   Average   Good   Outstanding

Media/Visuals
_____ **Points**

10   11   12   13   14   15   16   17   18   19   20
Awful   Poor   Average   Good   Outstanding

Delivery
_____ **Points**

1   2   3   4   5   6   7   8   9   10
Awful   Poor   Average   Good   Outstanding

General Comments

Critiqued by _____   **Total Points** _____ **(50)**

Moving into Multimedia

E xactly what is multimedia? The term can have two completely different meanings. One meaning is the use of multiple presentation media. With this definition, you can consider yourself using multimedia if you use an overhead projector for transparencies on one projection screen and also project slides on a second screen. You might use the overhead transparencies on one screen to show an outline of titles identifying pictures or other information that is being projected on the other screen.

A variation of this type of multimedia is when more images are shown simultaneously on a screen. Entertainment centers or amusement parks frequently put slide shows together using a dozen or more slide projectors with dissolve units to blend a multitude of pictures together. A tape recorder may be used to provide sound during the slide presentation.

Because of technology, a whole new meaning for multimedia has evolved. Multimedia is a computer product, activity, or application using text and graphic elements, color, sound, video, and animation. Viewers may be passive or interactive.

In a sense, movies and videotapes are true forms of multimedia; but they have been created in production studios with expensive equipment and crews—in an analog form. However, digital video brings video to the desktop. It lets users create, edit, store, retrieve, present,

This last chapter takes a look at multimedia–what it is and its place in the future. A description of MacroMind Director, a popular multimedia software program, is given at the end of the chapter.

and distribute multimedia information as electronic documents of bits and bytes, without any generational loss in transferring the data. For instance, Apple's QuickTime lets you put full-motion video into a word processing, spreadsheet, or desktop-published document by cutting and pasting–a procedure as easy as cutting and pasting clip art.

William L. Coggshall, president of New Media Research, Inc., classifies multimedia as different from the presentations previously described in this book with the following words:

> What we're doing is that if it moves or makes noise, we'll consider it a multimedia presentation, and if it doesn't, we'll call it a traditional presentation (Tony Reveaux, *Computer Currents*, August, 1991).

Multimedia Makeup

Because the integral parts of multimedia are text and graphics, color, sound, animation, video, and possibly interactivity, each of these areas requires examination

Apple and IBM have created a joint venture (known as Kaleida) to create a standard, interactive-media scripting language based on IBM's MediaScript, which would serve as the "PostScript of multimedia" by providing device independence. MediaScript will run on all platforms, including DOS. The scripting language will be supported by a platform-independent, system-software layer that includes QuickTime. This layer can be thought of as a multimedia operating system that will run on all computers, as well as on consumer "media player" machines (Bove and Rhodes, 1992).

to understand the total makeup or components of multimedia.

Text and Graphics

You have learned how to use text and graphics to develop visuals with your computer. The text and graphics remained on the screen as static pictures. By being able to create well-designed visuals with the computer, you are ready to incorporate the next steps of multimedia. Software programs that incorporate the ability to render three-dimensional drawings make pictures even more realistic.

Color

Previously, you have been told to limit the color on visuals to three or four colors. If you are using black-and-white clip art, you could painstakingly color the picture in a method similar to using crayons and a coloring book. Applying too many colors to a visual can be distracting and look "overdone."

Yet, you have 16.7 million colors available on the computer. This wide assortment of colors comes into play when you work with photo-realistic color images, which have 24 bits of color per pixel. These continuous-tone color images give the screen a real-world look. Full-color clip art is available, or you can use a color scanner to digitize full-color pictures into computer files. These techniques, therefore, violate the three- or four-color rule that gives an artificially applied look. Instead, they provide a full-color, realistic look.

Sound

Many computers (including all Macintosh models) can handle sound. If sound is not part of your computer system, add-on equipment makes it possible on newer models. Thus, sound is input directly into a presentation by using either prerecorded sound or by recording your own sounds.

If sound is used in a multimedia presentation, it should serve a purpose. Typical ways sound adds to a presentation are by using narration, voice-overs, sound effects, or music to go with an animated sequence or transition. An example is how music enhances cartoons to build a feeling of suspense or joy.

Off-the-shelf audio compact, CD-ROM, or laser optical disks can be used to provide sound for a multimedia program. Or, you can record digital sound either from audio equipment or with microphones, using a recorder and digitizer. Any sounds stored in digital format can be edited, altered, and copied with no loss in quality. You also can use a microcomputer to create and play digital sound with musical instruments and synthesizers.

Sound plays back with medium fidelity. By using a coprocessor card, you can have a high-fidelity, digital playback sound. Speakers are helpful in projecting the sound out into a room.

Animation

Many of the presentation programs used to make computer-generated productions described earlier in the book provide the capability for animated transitions between slides. One slide will dissolve into another in a variety of techniques such as wipe, fade, rain, or blinds.

In addition, some of the software programs allow you to create animation by adding items to a bullet chart in a build series, adding a sparkle to something on the chart, or zooming in a title. These programs only touch on the possibilities in the multimedia world.

The technique of animation is to make hundreds of drawings. When these drawings are projected sequentially onto a screen at a constant speed, they provide the illusion of movement. Rather than hiring dozens of artists to draw or paint hundreds and thousands of pictures, a computer can create animation. For instance, if you want a bird to fly across your monitor, you can create a sequence of, perhaps, only four different images of the bird flapping its wings.

However, when you place the bird on the screen in the proper sequence, imitating the positions of how it would raise and lower its wings, you can then use an in-between command to make the movement smooth. The effect is a bird flying for a short distance. By cutting and pasting this sequence several times, you can have the bird flutter across the screen. No one will be aware that you only used four different images to create the illusion of a complete flight.

Animation has a widespread range varying from either caricatures without a lot of detail to extremely fine, intricately detailed pictures. Many times, a concept is illustrated better without taking the extra time and money for intricate details.

Creating animation is the art of making movies on your desktop. The results can range from amateurish to professional, depending upon the time and talent of

By using a series of pictures, you create a moving effect. Powerful programs allow you to make birds fly and people walk or run.

the developer and the sophistication of hardware and software. Since you have complete control of animation, you may find it more effective for some purposes than video.

Video

Video is a technique that can capture and focus attention on a sequence of images. It allows you to present complex information from a variety of different locations in a simple and quick way.

Rather than hiring a camera crew with professional equipment, video can be created on a microcomputer—hence, the term desktop video. A camcorder is used to capture scenes from real life; a videocassette recorder serves the same purpose if you want to record from a television program. Remember that copyright laws apply, and official permission is needed. This footage can be edited into a video clip to be used with multimedia software.

Many times you may not want an entire video clip but only a single frame. A video digitizer is useful for capturing images from a video source, or a frame grabber can capture a sequence of video images.

Once a multimedia program is developed on a computer, a videotape recording of the presentation can be made. Such a recording is possible by using a video card on the computer to output the signal onto the videotape. The limitation of recording to a videotape is that interactivity between the videotape and the listener is not possible. However, a presenter using this type of media could stop the video to allow discussion or interactivity.

Interactivity

Presentations described thus far in this book have been of a linear type, although some interactivity or audience participation is possible. A big advantage of multimedia is that programs can be designed to allow a viewer to progress through a series of events in a nonlinear progression based upon responses and directions given by the viewer.

Interactive programs consist of a type of artificial intelligence in which branching is possible based upon the selection the viewer makes. A viewer's method of interaction with a multimedia program is by menu choices or dialog boxes that link and allow browsing in a non-structured way. Interactivity allows people to interact with and navigate through information.

People like to be involved actively rather than sit as passive observers. A presentation can be tailored to the observers' interests, needs, and learning speeds.

One state-of-the-art example of how this works is a shopping-mall directory. Rather than looking through an alphabetical list to find a store you want to shop in, you can use a videotext directory that asks you questions. Based upon your answers, the directory will indicate the particular type of store or stores you want. A diagram on the screen may even show you the best route to take to get to the store or stores.

Uses of Multimedia

One obvious use of multimedia is to enhance presentations. Multimedia can be quite time consuming, and its use requires additional software and hardware. It has found its way into a variety of useful applications within a short time span. These applications can be classified as business, education and training, and entertainment.

Business

Areas in business where multimedia is used effectively are sales and information kiosks. For example, an exhibit at a convention could have a multimedia program running on a computer. People could go through the program at their own pace by answering questions or interacting with the computer. Another application is for small group presentations. The group can observe and reach a consensus on what to input back to the computer; however, only one person at a time can interact unless a computer is provided for every participant.

Rather than sending out a booklet on their new Buick, General Motors sent a computer disk to people expressing an interest in seeing their new car by this method. The program displayed the car on the screen and allowed the viewer to get a full rundown on the car by pointing the computer mouse at various parts of the car or dialog boxes shown on the screen.

Education and Training

Education and business have both found that using multimedia programs can be an effective method of bringing new concepts to learners. Rather than becoming bored with a group-lockstep approach, people can progress through the information at their own individual rates. Workers in industrial or scientific settings can progress at a convenient rate and at an appropriate time.

Entertainment

The entertainment world has been a prime user of multimedia. Video games and computer programs can capture a person's attention for hours and hours; yet, the person will claim that time seemed to stand still. The ability of such programs to keep the attention span of individuals is in itself a demonstration of the effectiveness of multimedia.

The Future of Multimedia

Multimedia means new relationships. People in all walks of life are suddenly brought together. An interdisciplinary approach is needed for subjects such as art, business, and communication.

Multimedia is the booming new growth area for personal computers in the nineties. Newer and more powerful computers make multimedia a front-runner in this communications age.

The following statistics illustrate the expected growth in the area of multimedia for the next few years:

✔ Electronic frames, called on-screen glimpses or shows, is a growth area. In 1989, 59 million frames were produced. The number is expected to reach 284 million frames by 1993. New Media Research, Inc., calculates the opportunity gain for the multimedia industry–new products being sold–as $.4 billion in 1989, with 1993 projections increasing to $11.14 billion (Coggshall, personal communication, July, 1990).

✔ Computer animation is another strong growth area. According to the Roncarelli Report, the global value of computer animation totalled $1.4 billion in 1989 and is expected to reach $3.2 billion by 1993 (*Presentation Products Magazine*, October, 1990).

Rapid growth projections such as these emphasize the need for education and training in using multimedia. Although multimedia may be costly in the short run and requires new skills, it may prove to be the most cost effective of any type of presentation. Personal and professional presentations will continue to be affected by the incorporation of multimedia into both education and business.

MacroMind Director

MacroMind Director is probably the best known and also the most sophisticated multimedia-software program on the market. The software is available for Macintosh computers or the PC Windows platform. Software is available that will allow users to run a show that was developed on the Macintosh on either the Macintosh or the Windows platform.

How long has MacroMind been around?

MacroMind Director was created in 1985 as a program called VideoWorks. It created on-screen animation and was designed as a tool for education and fun. However, the company soon realized they had a product capable of serving in business as a visualization tool for communications and learning. Technical professionals could implement their ideas with a minimum amount of expense.

How can the program really be used in business?

The general purpose of MacroMind Director is for use in designing and producing dazzling presentations for an audience. Product demos or kiosks and education or training programs are examples of what can be created. Full-motion video with text overlays are possible, such as those used in television advertising, weather forecasting, and football broadcasting. The opportunities are unlimited.

What basic functions are performed?

MacroMind Director performs all the tasks of a full multimedia package—text and graphics, color, sound, animation, and interactivity. To picture what a multimedia program looks like, you could visualize a good colorful slide show full of graphics with movement and sound added.

What types of users can benefit from this program?

Small, medium, and large companies can all benefit from a product that enables getting the job done quickly, inexpensively, and at the last minute, while retaining control over the information. These reasons created the popularity of desktop publishing—the main difference in the final product is a using multimedia presentation rather than camera-ready, printed copy.

How does the program work?

MacroMind Director is a very sophisticated program, and you will not become proficient in all aspects of it overnight. However, you can get involved in the program at three different levels. Therefore, you could start with simple productions and advance into higher levels. An explanation of what can be done at each of these three levels is as follows:

Overview. The beginning level is *Overview.* You can create text effects by using a sparkle, letter slide, or typewriter effect. Zooming in or out on text, such as a title, is possible. Animated bullet and bar charts attract attention as they move onto the screen. To control the pace of the program, you can either set timers or use a mouse click to advance to the next screen—allowing you to coordinate the screen images with your talk. Sound effects and even short film loops can be added. Transitions from one screen to the next add interesting effects such as dissolves, reveals, strips, venetian or vertical blinds, wipes, and zooms. The presentation is run by a control panel with commands similar to an audio or video recorder—play, stop, rewind, step backwards, step forward, etc. Keyboard shortcuts also can be used to control the presentation.

Studio. In *Studio*, you are really directing a movie. The screen becomes a stage. You bring in a cast–consisting of a window showing a tiny thumbnail representation of each cast member. Cast members can include graphics, scanned images, pieces of graphics and scanned images, text, individual letters, sounds, custom color palettes, and even film loops. Each moving figure consists of numerous cast members–one for each shape, position, and size. A score window shows channels as rows, and frames as columns, and is used to describe the animation over time. You direct your movie by inserting cast members and other directives on the score.

Interactive. The *Interactive* phase of MacroMind Director uses a scripting language called Lingo to direct the program. Scripts, sprites, puppets, buttons, and macros are all controlled by the Lingo scripting. A user responds by clicking on a selected button–either by using the mouse or a touch-sensitive screen. Thus, the user progresses in a branching versus a linear manner.

What hardware is required for MacroMind Director?
MacroMind Director is compatible with all Macintosh computers and IBM compatibles using Windows. Depending on the length and complexity of your creations, however, you will need lots of RAM and storage capabilities.

–JK

References

Bove, Tony, and Rhodes, Cheryl. (January-February, 1992). "Will the Real Multimedia Please Stand Up?" *Desktop, IV*, 37-38.

Coggshall, William L. (July, 1990). Personal communication with author.

"Newsworthy." (October, 1990). *Presentation Products Magazine*, 8.

Reveaux, Tony. (August, 1991). *Computer Currents*, 20.

Afterword

You have acquired the basic knowledge to create high-impact business presentations. You can create an image that makes the difference. Now it is time to start.

Because you have read this book, you are aware of the many possibilities for developing and designing your presentation. You, as the presenter, need to get personally involved in creating your presentation. While others might help in the final production stage, only you can develop the message you truly want to convey–in just the way you intend. Seek advice from others when you need it, but you should plan your strategy, select your media, develop your message, and design your visuals. Your involvement will pay off when you stand in front of a group and can speak with complete confidence because you know your material like the back of your hand. Your sense of accomplishment can build your enthusiasm, too.

For those instances when you need additional help, you are now familiar with the terminology and capabilities to better communicate with graphic artists, vendors, and service bureau personnel.

To aid you, a glossary of presentation terms is provided in the appendix. Also, presentation software, hardware, magazines, and other special resources are listed. While these lists are certainly not all-inclusive,

In today's competitive world, keeping up with the growth of technology is important. Creating high-impact presentations will help you advance in your career.

they will acquaint you with many top-quality companies you might contact for additional information about their products. New ones are being released daily.

Technology Growth

Two trends always seem to occur when technology becomes more popular—the cost becomes more affordable and the technology becomes easier to use. When you realize that desktop publishing began in 1985 and the first presentation software was released in 1987, you can truly understand how new these capabilities are. And, yet, the improved output in printed material and presentation capabilities is having, and will continue to have, a profound effect on communication in business.

Advancing technology is rapidly making new software and hardware developments available. What was once the norm is now mediocre—our expectations of what it takes to create a high-impact presentation are changing. You need to pull together everything at your disposal to make those few minutes in front of your group achieve the results you need.

Jonathan Seybold, President of Seybold Publication, believes the computing industry is shifting its focus from data processing to gathering, analyzing, and organizing information (Castro, 1990). Organized information must be shared, and technological advancements in the fields of desktop presentations and publishing make this sharing more effective and communication more successful.

Even though the development and use of media increases costs, the added expense can prove cost effective. Thomas Milton, a senior fellow at the Socio-Economic Research Institute of America, believes the economic slump and political uncertainty in many parts of the world increase the need for greater productivity in all sectors of the economy. He thinks society will fuel the growth of presentation products and accelerate the integration of the various technologies. The following reasons for this growth increase were cited:

✔ Rising gasoline and aviation fuel prices make teleconferencing a very attractive alternative to face-to-face meetings. Conversely, the rising costs of bringing people together for meetings demands that the sessions achieve maximum productivity.

✔ Layoffs and factory closures require worker retraining—a perfect job for interactive technology.

✔ In the face of funding cutbacks, schools must improve their effectiveness. Presentation systems can broaden the reach of the teacher and add new dimensions to the learning experience.

✔ The growing problem of health care will create the need for learning systems to educate and motivate people to take responsibility for their health (Lindstrom, 1990, December, p. 8).

Career Advancement

We believe presentation skills can advance you in your career—whatever it may be. The ability to organize your thoughts, conceptualize how you will communicate your thoughts, and then think on your feet in front of people is a tremendous asset in most any career. Yet, this ability is not something all people possess.

Often students in college are required to make presentations in classes, but few receive training in how technology can help them in making their presentations. Even in business communication classes, the subject of oral reports or presentations may not be emphasized. The authors' analysis of 17 popular college business communication textbooks shows that an average of only 4.31 percent of the pages are devoted to the topic of oral presentations.

Students recognize the need and are eager to learn more. In a survey of graduate MBA students at California Polytechnic State University (Carter, 1992), 63 percent of the employed students (representing five class sections) completing a newly developed course titled *Professional Presentations Using Technology* currently use the presentation skills acquired in the class and 100 percent believe that they will use them in the future. The students strongly recommended that the course be required during the first year in the graduate program. Many students felt the course should also be required as a part of the undergraduate curriculum.

So, regardless of your experience–whether you are a new entrant into the workforce or a "seasoned" professional–you can use the available technology and processes outlined in this book to be a better communicator. You can create professional presentations with the image you want and the impact you need. We wish you success!

References

Carter, Kristin Dee. (1992). "A Study of the Impact of the Graduate Course *Professional Presentations Using Technology*." Unpublished thesis, California State Polytechnic University, Pomona.

Castro, Christine. (November, 1990). "Jonathan Seybold Examines the Foundation for Change." *Computer Publishing Magazine, 5,* 21.

Lindstrom, Robert. (December, 1990). "Podium." *Presentation Products Magazine,* 8.

Glossary

3-D The three-dimensional illusion of depth for bar, pie, or line charts created by shading. Presentation software provides default values which can be easily modified to change the appearance of the bars or pie segments.

35 mm slides Slides produced with photographic film in 35 millimeter gauge. Slides are created by using presentation software to output computer images to a film recorder. They are developed as any other slides, provide vivid color for presentation visuals, and contribute to a very professional-looking presentation.

Accent lighting Directional lighting to provide a focus on one area of a room.

Acoustics The structural and decorative features of a room that determine how well sound can be heard.

Agenda Detailed information about a scheduled meeting such as beginning/ending times, date, place, topics, and responsibilities.

Alignment Arrangement or positioning of type elements with respect to left and right margins (flush left, centered, flush right, or justified).

Creating high-impact presentations of today requires an understanding of terminology from the areas of audio-visual, communication, graphic design, computers, and computer graphics. This appendix provides a glossary of words used throughout the book.

Ambient lighting   The general, overall illumination in a room.

Animation   The capability of presentation and multimedia software to create illusions of movement.

Area chart   A filled-in line chart. See *Line chart.*

Articulation   The act of saying words distinctly and clearly.

Ascender   The part of a type character (b, d, f, h, k, l, and t) extending above the height of a lowercase x.

Audio-visual presentation   A presentation in which a speaker uses visual images of some type to help convey the presentation message.

Balance   A sense of equilibrium in the design. Balance can be formal (where all images and/or text are arranged symmetrically) or informal (where images and/or text are arranged asymmetrically). Informal balance provides the greatest design flexibility.

Bar chart   A single-scale graph drawn with parallel bars used to compare quantities at a specific time or to show the quantity variance of something over time.

Baseline   The imaginary line on which the bottom of letters rest.

Bit   The basic unit of numbering in a binary numbering system (binary digit).

Bit-mapped   Images (pictures or fonts) made up of individual dots, as opposed to lines or other shapes.

Borders   A line or pattern used around the edge of a visual to add a consistent look to a series of visuals in a presentation.

Brightness   The intensity of color.

Build series   A variation of a bullet list in which each item is highlighted as discussion progresses. Usually the completed items remain on the visual in a dimmed color while the current item is highlighted in a brighter color.

Bullet list   A vertical list with items introduced by small graphic symbols (such as a bullet, arrow, box, etc.) that set them apart from each other.

Camcorder   A camera that records video.

Canned art   See *Clip art.*

CD-ROM   See *Compact disk.*

Chart junk   Too much information or graphic enhancements which cause the meaning of a chart to be distorted and difficult to understand.

Climatization   Heating, ventilation, and air conditioning systems (HVAC) combined to help control the interior climate for the comfort of the people in a room.

Clip art   Illustrations available commercially; now available on computer disk for easy retrieval of black-and-white or full-color images. Most vendors usually provide a hard copy of the illustrations. The term "clip art" is a carry over from the days when these illustrations were available only on paper and designers literally cut out the illustrations with scissors and pasted them on their page layouts. Today, graphic file formats for the illustrations must be compatible with desktop publishing, word processing, or presentation software being used.

Cluster seating   A seating arrangement suitable for small-group discussion with usually four to six people in a cluster.

Clustered bar chart   A group of bars that represent similar items from different data sets. These charts are effective for making comparisons.

Color   The reflection or absorption of light by a particular surface.

Column bar chart   See *Vertical bar chart*.

Compact disk (*CD*)   A plastic disk that uses optical storage technology to store digital data as microscopic pits and smooth areas which reflect light differently. Most disks presently in use provide read-only memory; they are referred to as CD-ROM disks.

Computer conference   An electronic meeting between people sending messages via a computer network (computers cabled together or connected through telephone lines).

Computer-based screen show A presentation in which text and graphic images are displayed on a computer; with a projection device, the images can be projected to a large screen for group viewing. Interesting effects can be added to control how the images advance from one screen to another. Also referred to as computer-generated shows.

Computer-generated visual Any visual prepared with a computer using presentation software.

Content outline A list of topics arranged in the most logical sequence for a presentation.

Coprocessor card A microprocessor support chip optimized for a specific processing operation.

Copyboard A board used to record, display, and reproduce whatever is written upon it. This is an excellent meeting management device to capture participants' ideas in brainstorming and planning sessions.

Critical path method chart A process diagram showing the chronological succession of project activities.

Decibel A measure of sound intensity.

Descender The part of a type character (g, j, p, q, and y) extending below the baseline of a lowercase x.

Desktop presentations Visual presentations prepared on a desktop computer system (computer, laser printer or other output devices, and presentation software). Presentation software provides automatic sizing for slides or overheads, word processing capabilities, drawing and graphic features, and development and projection of computer-based screen shows.

Desktop publishing   The process of producing publication-quality materials such as brochures, catalogs, books, etc. with a desktop computer system (computer, laser printer, and page layout software). This process allows a level of printing sophistication formerly possible only by professional typesetting and graphic design artists.

Desktop video   Video production using low-cost video equipment and desktop computers.

Deviation bar chart   A chart with bars to the left or right of the reference axis indicating the area of standard deviation. Also used to emphasize differences from an expected value.

Diagrams   Images showing either spatial relationships or process paths.

Dialog box   An on-screen message box used in some software to convey or request information from the user.

Digital sound   Sound created using a computer.

Digitize   To turn an image (artwork, photographs, text) into a format usable by a computer system through a process that scans the image into digital bits.

Dingbat   A decorative character or symbol (such as a star, flower, pointing hand) used for bulleted lists, borders, or decoration.

Dissolve effect   A transition technique in computer-based presentations for changing one computer visual to another by having the existing visual appear to dissolve on the screen.

Enunciation   The act of saying words that are complete and easy-to-understand; avoidance of mumbling and slurring words.

Ergonomics   The study of relationships between individuals and the environment.

Evaluation feedback   Audience reaction to a presentation. This can be obtained informally by observing responses and attitudes of the audience or formally by using an evaluation form.

Exploding pie chart   A pie chart with emphasis added to one segment by visually pulling it away from the whole. See *Pie chart.*

Fade effect   A transition technique in computer-based presentations for changing one computer visual to another by having the existing visual appear to fade off the screen.

Film recorder   A device with a camera used to expose film to make slides of computer images for a presentation. When using presentation software, a film recorder is one available output device.

Flatbed scanner   A type of scanner with a glass plate similar to a photocopy machine on which the image to be scanned is placed. See *Scanner.*

Flip chart   A large paper tablet, usually placed on an easel, suitable for use in presenting to small groups. Flip charts may be prepared during a presentation, or can be created in advance using a computer, software, and printing devices to make professional-looking visuals.

Floor plan   A diagram showing drafted or architectural drawings prepared to scale for a room or building arrangement. Often developed with computer-aided design software.

Flowchart   A process diagram used to show the sequence of steps involved in a project.

Flush-left alignment   Text that is aligned at the left margin but ragged (uneven) at the right margin.

Flush-right alignment   Text that is aligned at the right margin but ragged (uneven) at the left margin.

Font   A set of characters (the full alphabet, numbers, and symbols) in one weight and style of a typeface. See *Typeface.*

Footcandle   A unit of measurement used to determine light density.

Formal balance   A centered pattern of images on a page or visual arranged to be symmetrical and appear dignified.

Frame   An individual slide, overhead transparency, or film image. See *Borders*.

Frame grabber   A device used to capture one or more video images.

Front projection   The capability of equipment within a room (such as a slide projector or ceiling-mounted unit) that projects presentation visuals on a large screen for audience viewing.

Gantt chart   A process diagram representing activities occurring either sequentially or concurrently along a time line.

Glass beaded surface   A projection screen surface that provides superior brightness, greater picture depth, richer detail, and excellent tone gradation in a normally darkened room. This surface is suitable for slide or movie projections.

Gradient color   The gradual change of one color to another with no discernible break; also called *graduated* or *ramped color*.

Graduated color   See *Gradient color*.

Graphics   Image enhancements such as lines, boxes, backgrounds, art, clip art, scanned images, etc., used to create interesting and appealing visuals.

Gray-scale scanner   A type of scanner that uses variable values for different shades of gray. See *Scanner*.

Grid   A pattern of evenly spaced, intersecting lines on a chart showing scale and reference values. A grid may also be used like graph paper on a screen as an aid for alignment while developing visuals.

Group decision support system   Computer systems and software designed to facilitate group input and decision making.

Group lockstep approach   A teaching method frequently used in software and computer training when participants follow the direction of a trainer and perform each process collectively. One drawback to this method is that the entire group could be held back by the difficulties of one participant; lesson progression is limited to the slowest participant in the group.

Handouts   Printed materials used during a presentation. Appearance is very important. Distribution timing depends on the purpose and desired audience interaction.

Herringbone pattern   A seating arrangement where tables and chairs for participants are arranged in V shapes with tables angled.

Horizontal bar chart   A chart with one scale used to show relationships or a single point in time. Usually ranked by size with the largest bar on top.

Hue   The actual name used for the color of an object (such as red or blue); however, the perception of hue is affected by background or surrounding colors.

Importing   Transferring a single image or a complete file from one document to another using one or more computer programs.

Informal balance   A random, uneven pattern of images on a page or visual. The contrast of images forms a pleasing and interesting arrangement. Informal balance provides more flexibility in design than formal balance.

Interactive program   A multimedia program that allows the user choices to direct the activities of the program. For example, once the user makes a decision from a menu or dialog box, a particular branch of the program is followed.

Justified   Text aligned on both left and right margins (flush-left/flush-right alignment). Spacing between words and letters is adjusted so all lines begin and end in the same positions and paragraphs have a blocked look.

Kerning   The adjustment of space between paired letters. While software provides automatic kerning, sometimes adjustment to particular letter spacing is necessary to improve the appearance and readability of text—especially when text is enlarged for headlines and titles.

Kiosk   An interactive multimedia information booth.

Label   Text annotation identifying the title, subtitle, and variables of a chart.

Landscape   A page orientation where printing is aligned horizontally on the long edge of the paper (for standard size paper, the 11-inch side is at the top). See *Portrait.*

Laser optical disk   A device used for the storage and retrieval of still pictures or video pictures and sound.

Lavaliere-type mike   A small microphone which can be clipped to clothing; usually equipped with a long cord to allow mobility when speaking.

LCD panel   A liquid crystal display, flat-panel unit connected to a computer and placed on an overhead projector. The projector light shines through the LCD panel to show the computer's screen image. These units can project in black and white or in full color.

Lead time   The time before a presentation that is available for planning and production of needed materials.

Leading   The vertical spacing between lines of text, measured in *points.*

Legend   A caption or notation explaining the meaning of colors or patterns used in a chart.

Lightness   A quality of color determined by how much white, gray, or black is in the hue.

Line chart   A chart used to illustrate trends (usually over time) by connecting data points with curved or straight lines. Charts may show a comparison of several trends by using multiple lines differentiated by color or line styles.

Line spacing See *Leading.*

Map A place diagram showing a map. This could be any type of map from detailed directional maps to maps showing the outline of a country or nation. Sometimes map diagrams are used as a background image with numeric charts displayed in the foreground.

Master See *Template.*

Matte surface An all-purpose surface for projection screens that is less expensive than glass beaded or pearlescent surfaces.

Media Communication devices used to support and help convey a presentation message. Media takes many forms ranging from simple (such as an overhead transparency or a handout) to complex (such as a computer-based or multimedia presentation).

Miniatures Copies of visuals reduced in size and arranged on handouts for notetaking.

Minutes Written documentation of the decisions, accomplishments, etc., of a meeting.

Model An actual product or miniature scaled mock-up that closely resembles the real product.

Modem   A device that transfers digital computer signals to analog signals for transmission over telephone lines. Another modem on the receiving end transfers signals back to digital.

Modified classroom   A seating arrangement where tables and chairs for participants are arranged in a semicircular arrangement. Tables are often connected with trapezoid pieces for a smooth, continuous appearance. Rooms may be tiered for maximum visibility.

Modulation   A change in the tone or pitch of the voice.

Multimedia presentations   Visual presentations that integrate text, graphics, sound, animation, video, and interactivity to communicate information and express imagination to an audience.

Nonverbal communication   Body language, including mannerisms and gestures, which conveys messages.

Numeric chart   A chart used to convey information and concepts to audiences by showing the relative proportions of data sets. These charts show frequency distributions, time-related events, comparisons, or correlations.

Optical disk   See *Compact disk.*

Organizational chart   A diagram used in presentations for illustrating hierarchical relationships such as a company structure.

Overhead transparencies   Plastic sheets printed with text, graphics, or pictures, allowing an image to be projected to a screen by means of an overhead projector. Also referred to as view graphs, foils, or overheads.

Paint program   Software that enables the user to draw. Drawing tools represented by various paint object icons (such as a brush or spray can) are used to color the on-screen pixels in different colors. Images are treated as a collection of pixels rather than objects or shapes.

Paired horizontal bars   Bars in a chart used to compare negative/positive sets of data. Usually negative values are placed on the left of a reference point and positive values are placed on the right.

Parallel structure   The consistent sequencing of words within paragraphs, series of sentences, or lists. For example, if some phrases begin with verbs, then all phrases in a list should begin with verbs; if some begin with nouns, then all should begin with nouns. Also important for consistency in titles and subtitles.

Pearlescent surface   A projection screen surface which has excellent reflectivity and brilliance. This surface is useful for video and liquid crystal display projection.

PERT chart   A type of chart used for management planning, showing the correct order of events and activities in a particular project.

Pictorial symbols   Images used to represent the value or exact size of a bar. May include pictures, symbols, or other objects.

Pie chart   A type of chart that contains a single-scaled, circular graphic that shows proportions in relation to a whole.

Pixels   The tiny dots of light (picture elements) that form characters and objects on a computer monitor. The clarity of the monitor is determined by the pixel resolution (the density of the pixels).

Place diagram   A diagram which displays spatial relationships.

Point   The smallest typographic unit of measurement for typefaces and lines. One inch contains 72 points.

Portrait   A page orientation where printing is aligned vertically on the short edge of the paper (for standard size paper, the 8 1/2-inch side is at the top). See *Landscape.*

Posters   Thick, oversized pieces of paper. Posters can be prepared during a presentation or can be made in advance using a computer, software, and printing devices to make professional-looking printed visuals.

Presentation graphics   High-quality slides, overhead transparencies, or computer images for displaying information to an audience. The term may be used to represent specific programs that create graphs. See *Desktop presentations.*

Presentation media   The combination of written materials and projected visual images used in a presentation. This is a term coined by Apple Computer, Inc., to encompass both the areas of desktop publishing and desktop presentations.

Presentation strategy   A crucial part of presentation planning that includes audience analysis, time consideration, resource availability, objectives, research, and presentation organization.

Preview   The process of checking before a presentation to see that slides or other materials are arranged in proper sequence.

Process diagram   A diagram showing sequential, branching, or concurrent steps in a procedure from its beginning to end.

Projection unit   A direct computer-to-projector system for displaying computer-based presentations which allows vivid, full-color projection. The units may be mobile units (which look similar to large-screen televisions) or ceiling-mounted devices which project to a wall-mounted screen.

Ragged   Lines of text (ragged-left or ragged-right alignment) beginning or ending at uneven positions.

RAM   Random Access Memory. The volatile memory of a computer system that is operating when the system is on and inactive when the system is off.

Ramped color   See *Gradient color.*

Rear projection   The capability of equipment to project images from behind the wall at the focal point of the presentation room. Only the visual, not the equipment, is visible for audience viewing.

Rehearse   To practice a presentation by actually going through the materials and giving the presentation.

Review   To go over notes before a presentation in order to study pertinent facts or figures.

Rule   A horizontal or vertical line of varying width, texture, and color.

Sans serif   Typeface characters designed without serifs (small strokes on the ends of the main character stems).

Saturation   The brightness and vividness of a color.

Scale   Numbering on the axes of a chart. Should be in units easily understood by the readers/viewers.

Scale drawing   A place diagram representing the representative relational scale of an object or site.

Scanner   A device that digitizes an image (artwork, photographs, or text) and stores it as a computer file. The use of optical character recognition software is necessary to interpret the scanned image as text.

Scattergram   A chart showing the correlation between two data sets. Points are plotted on two independent scales and tested statistically with regression analysis.

Close proximity of plotted points indicates a high correlation; point dispersion indicates low correlation. Also called dot chart.

Screening   Various densities of black-and-white patterns used to create an illusion of different shades of gray.

Seating cone   The area of a room where seated participants can view a projection screen.

Serif   Fine cross strokes or flares at the ends of a letter's main stems.

Sheet-fed scanner   A device that requires the image to pass through the scanning equipment. This unit can only work with sheet thicknesses and is inappropriate for scanning from a book or other large object. See *Scanner*.

Stacked bar chart   A bar chart which combines related values into columns, then compares columns representing different data sets. While this chart is effective for comparing the total column values, it does not effectively show the related values which make up the columns.

Storyboard   A visual outline of a presentation showing sketched layouts of images to be developed with the computer using presentation software. The images can be sketched on paper or on note cards by hand to allow easy rearranging. Some software allows the display of multiple images on the screen at one time in miniature form to aid in creating storyboards with a computer.

Task lighting   Illumination of a visual task area, such as a lectern, for improved visibility of notes.

Telephone conference   An audio conference between two or more people at potentially remote locations.

Template   An image that serves as a background for computer-based presentations. Templates add consistency and continuity and may include such elements as the presentation title, a company logo, line art, or graphics. While templates can easily be created, presentation software provides many predesigned templates which also can be customized.

Thermofax   A machine which uses a heat process to make overhead transparencies.

Tick mark   A mark used to call attention to detail, to indicate value, or to serve as a division in a grid.

Time line   A line plotted in a diagram or graph designed to show historical progress.

Title visual   The opening visual in a presentation. It serves the same purpose as a title page of a report and includes such things as title of the presentation, presenter's name, corporate logo, etc.

Tone   The mood of a presentation. Subdued colors may contribute to a conservative tone; bright, bold colors may convey a mood of excitement. Content, clip art, and other graphic enhancements will help to set the tone of visuals, and visuals will set the tone of the presentation.

Tool box   A group of icons (miniature illustrations representing a function) visible on a computer screen with some presentation software. The user selects an appropriate icon to perform a particular software function such as drawing squares, circles, curved lines, or changing colors.

Tracking   The overall spacing within text. Tracking is often adjusted, especially for headlines and titles, when spacing between letters appears uneven.

Type   See *Typeface.*

Type family   All the variations of a basic type design in every weight and point size.

Type style   Individual variations of a typeface, such as plain, bold, italic, underscore, shadow, and outline.

Typeface   A specific type design, such as Times Roman or Garamond. Some people use the terms *typeface* and *font* interchangeably.

Typography   The art of producing words and symbols from type. Also, the terminology and rules for using different typefaces.

V-Shape pattern   A seating arrangement where tables and chairs for participants are arranged in a V shape with tables angled on both sides of a center aisle.

Vertical bar chart   A chart with bars forming vertical columns to show quantity relationships or how something changes over time.

Video clip   A section of video tape.

Video conference   An audio and video conference between two or more locations.

Video digitizer   A device that captures images in digital form from video tape.

Videocard   A special card in a computer connected to a video recorder which allows the conversion of computer images to videotape. Sound or voice-overs can be edited into the production with videocards.

Videoshow device   Equipment which allows the projection of visuals prepared as a computer-based show without the computer.

Visuals   Objects or projected images containing text, graphs, and illustrations used to clarify a presentation message.

Voice-overs   The audio portion of a multimedia program when a graphic or video is displayed and the speaker can be heard but not seen.

Wipe effect   A transition technique in computer-based presentations for changing one computer visual to another by having an existing visual appear to be wiped off the screen.

Word spacing   Horizontal spacing between words created by the spacebar on the keyboard. While this spacing is automatically set in relation to the typeface and size selected, it can be adjusted with some software.

X axis   The horizontal line of a chart showing independent data classification. It usually shows time stated in years, months, quarters, or weeks. (For a horizontal bar chart, see the *Y axis.*)

Y axis   The vertical line of a chart showing the values of the dependent variable data set. This is usually the focus of the chart. (For a horizontal bar chart, see *X axis.*)

Presentation Software

Desktop presentation software has special features to simplify the task of creating visuals for overhead transparencies, 35 mm slides, or computer-based screen shows. New products are continually being released.

Macintosh

Aldus Persuasion
Aldus Corporation
411 First Avenue S.
Seattle, WA 98104-2871
(206) 622-5500

Aperture Visual Information Manager
Graphic Management Group
100-3 Summit Lake Drive
Valhalla, NY 10595
(914) 769-7800

CA-Cricket Graph
CA-Cricket Presents
Computer Associates Intl., Inc.
711 Stewart Avenue
Garden City, NY 11530
(800) 645-6003

Data Desk
Data Description, Inc.
15 Lisa Lane
Ithaca, NY 14850
(607) 257-1000

DeltaGraph Professional
DeltaPoint, Inc.
2 Harris Ct., Ste. B1
Monterey, CA 93940
(800) 367-4334

Easy Slider III
Management Graphics, Inc.
1401 E. 79th Street
Minneapolis, MN 55425
(612) 854-1220

Freelance Graphics
Lotus Development Corp.
55 Cambridge Parkway
Cambridge, MA 02142
(800) 343-5414

Full Impact
Ashton-Tate Corporation
20101 Hamilton Avenue
Torrance, CA 90509
(800) 437-4329

GraphMaster
380 Interstate N. Parkway
Ste. 190
Atlanta, GA 30339
(404) 956-0325

ImageBoss 1000
RGB Technology, Inc.
6862 Elm Street
McLean, VA 22101
(703) 556-0667

InfoLynx
InfoTouch Marketing Corp.
120 Walton Street
Syracuse, NY 13202
(800) 966-5969

MacGraphX
Bravo Technologies, Inc.
P.O. Box 10078
Berkeley, CA 94709-0078
(510) 841-8552

Microsoft PowerPoint
Microsoft Corporation
One Microsoft Way
Redmond, WA 98052
(800) 426-9400

More
Symantec
10201 Torre Avenue
Cupertino, CA 95014
(408) 253-9600

On the Air
Meyer Software
616 Continental Road
Hatboro, PA 19040
(215) 675-3890

On-Command
Computer Support Corp.
15926 Midway Road
Dallas, TX 75244
(214) 661-8960

PosterWorks
S. H. Pierce & Company
One Kendall Square
Bldg. 600, Ste. 323
Cambridge, MA 02139
(617) 395-8350

PresentationPro
Strade Ware Corporation
1400 Market, Ste. 100
Denver, CO 80202
(303) 820-2020

Professional Image
Stokes Imaging Services
7000 Cameron Road
Austin, TX 78752
(512) 458-2201

Quickchart
Management Graphics, Inc.
1401 E. 79th Street
Minneapolis, MN 55425
(612) 854-1220

StrataFlight
Strata, Inc.
2 W. St. George Blvd.,
Ste. 2100
St. George, UT 84770
(800) 678-7282

Studio/1
Electronic Arts
1820 Gateway Drive
San Mateo, CA 94404
(415) 571-7171

PC

2-D Graphics
3-D Graphics
Intex Solutions, Inc.
161 Highland Avenue
Needham, MA 02194
(617) 449-6222

35mm Express
Business & Professional
Software, Inc.
139 Main Street
Cambridge, MA 02142
(800) 342-5277

Aldus Persuasion
Aldus Corporation
411 First Avenue S, Ste. 200
Seattle, WA 98104-2871
(206) 622-5500

Applause
Ashton-Tate Corporation
20101 Hamilton Avenue
Torrance, CA 90509-9972
(800) 437-4329

Batchprint
Pyxel Applications, Inc.
2917 Mohawk Drive
Richmond, VA 23235
(804) 320-5573

CA-Cricket Presents
Computer Associates Int., Inc.
711 Stewart Avenue
Garden City, NY 11530
(800) 645-6003

DB Graphics
Microrim, Inc.
15395 S.E. 30th Place
Bellevue, WA 98007-9918
(206) 649-9500

DeltaGraph Professional
DeltaPoint, Inc.
2 Harris Court, Ste. B1
Monterey, CA 93940
(800) 367-4334

DrawPerfect
WordPerfect Corporation
1555 N. Technology Way
Orem, UT 84057
(800) 321-3280

Energraphics
Enertronics Research, Inc.
1801 Beltway Drive
St. Louis, MO 63114
(800) 325-0174

Express Presenter
Power Up Software
Corporation
2929 Campus Drive
San Mateo, CA 94403
(800) 851-2917

Freelance Graphics
Lotus Development
Corporation
55 Cambridge Parkway
Cambridge, MA 02142
(800) 343-5414

Graph-in-the-Box Executive
New England Software, Inc.
Greenwich Office Park 3
Greenwich, CT 06831
(203) 625-0062

Graphics Gallery
Hewlett-Packard Company
Stevens Creek Blvd.
P.O. 58195
Santa Clara, CA 95025
(800) 752-0900

Harvard Graphics
Software Publishing Corp.
1901 Landings Drive
P.O. Box 7210
Mountain View, CA 94039
(415) 962-8910

Hollywood
Claris Corporation
5201 Patrick Henry Drive
Santa Clara, CA 95052
(408) 987-7000

Hotshot Presents
Symsoft Corporation
916 Southwood Blvd.
Ste. 1A/Call Box 5
Incline Village, NV 89450
(702) 832-4300

Image1 Plus
System Generation Associates, Inc.
122 N. Cortez, Ste. 305
Prescott, AZ 86301
(602) 778-4840

ImageStation
Yale Graphics
8220 Northcreek, Ste. 100
Cincinnati, OH 45236
(513) 791-9253

IMSI Graphics Pak
IMSI
1938 Fourth Street
San Rafael, CA 94901
(800) 833-4674

Keyboard Master M-1328
Apollo
60 Trade Zone Court
Ronkonkoma, NY 11779
(516) 467-8033

Kinetic Words, Graphs, & Art
Kinetic Presentations, Inc.
250 Distillery Commons
Louisville, KY 40206
(502) 583-1679

LaserKey
Electronic Arts
1820 Gateway Drive
San Mateo, CA 94404
(415) 571-7171

Micrografx Charisma
Micrografx, Inc.
1303 Arapaho Road
Richardson, TX 75081
(800) 733-3729

Microsoft PowerPoint
Microsoft Corporation
One Microsoft Way
Redmond, WA 98052
(800) 426-9400

OctoSplit
Communications Specialties,
Inc.
89A Cabot Court
Hauppauge, NY 11788
(516) 273-0404

On-Command
Computer Support
Corporation
15926 Midway Road
Dallas, TX 75244
(214) 661-8960

Panel Ready
Mind Path Technologies, Inc.
12700 Park Central Drive,
Ste. 1801
Dallas, TX 75251
(214) 233-9296

Picturelt
General Parametrics
Corporation
1250 Ninth Street
Berkeley, CA 94710
(800) 223-0999

Pixie
Zenographics, Inc.
4 Executive Circle, Ste. 200
Irvine, CA 92714
(800) 366-7494

Presentation Express
3-D Visions Corporation
2780 Skypark Drive
Torrance, CA 90505
(800) 729-4723

Presentation Maker
System Generation Associates,
Inc.
122 N. Cortez, Ste. 305
Prescott, AZ 86301
(602) 778-4840

Presentation Team
Digital Research, Inc.
Box DRI
70 Garden Court
Monterey, CA 93942
(408) 649-3896

Pyxel Visuals
Pyxel Applications, Inc.
2917 Mohawk Drive
Richmond, VA 23235
(804) 320-5573

QuadSplit
Communications Specialties,
Inc.
89A Cabot Court
Hauppauge, NY 11788
(516) 273-0404

Quantum Graphics
Threshold Software, Inc.
29 S. Park Avenue
Hinsdale, IL 60521
(708) 887-0480

Quickchart

Management Graphics, Inc.
1401 E. 79th Street
Minneapolis, MN 55425
(612) 854-1220

SlideWrite Plus
SlideWrite Presenter

Advanced Graphics Software,
Inc.
333 W. Maude Avenue
Ste. 105
Sunnyvale, CA 94086
(408) 749-8620

SoftCraft Presenter

SoftCraft, Inc.
16 N. Carroll Street, Ste. 500
Madison, WI 53703
(800) 351-0500

Stanford Graphics
Presentation & Analysis

Business & Professional
Software, Inc.
139 Main Street
Cambridge, MA 02142
(800) 342-5277

Trumpet Plus

Business & Professional
Software, Inc.
139 Main Street
Cambridge, MA 02142
(800) 342-5277

TwinSplit

Communications Specialties,
Inc.
89A Cabot Court
Hauppauge, NY 11788
(516) 273-0404

VCN Concorde

Visual Communications
Network, Inc.
238 Main Street
Cambridge, MA 02142
(617) 497-4000

VIS Presentation

Comteq USA
13949 Equitable Road
Cerritos, CA 90701
(800) 521-4892

Presentation Hardware

Color Printers

Agfa Corporation
1 Ramland Road
Orangeburg, NY 10962
(800) 227-2780

ALPS Electric USA, Inc .
3553 N. First Street
San Jose, CA 95134
(408) 432-6000

CalComp, Inc.
2411 W. LaPalma Avenue
Anaheim, CA 92803
(800) 932-1212

Canon USA, Inc.
One Canon Plaza
Lake Success, NY 11042-9979
(800) OK-CANON

Citizen America Corporation
2450 Broadway, Suite 600
Santa Monica, CA 90404-3060
(800) 556-1234

Colorocs Corporation
2805 Peterson Place
Norcross, GA 30071
(404) 840-6500

CSS Laboratories, Inc.
1641 McGraw Avenue
Irvine, CA 92714
(800) 966-2771

Dataproducts Corporation
6219 De Soto Avenue
Woodland Hills, CA
91365-0746
(818) 887-8000

Digital Equipment Corp.
Technology Park Drive
Westford, MA 01886
(800) 344-4825

Eastman Kodak Company
343 State Street
Rochester, NY 14650
(800) 344-0006

Epson America, Inc.
20770 Madrona Avenue
Torrance, CA 90509-2842
(800) 289-3776

Fujitsu America, Inc.
3055 Orchard Drive
San Jose, CA 95134-2022
(800) 626-4686

General Parametrics
1250 Ninth Street
Berkeley, CA 94710
(800) 223-0999

The market for presentation hardware is a quickly growing market as more and more technology becomes available. This section includes names, addresses, and phone numbers of a few of the many suppliers providing presentation technology.

Hewlett-Packard Company
19310 Pruneridge Avenue
Cupertino, CA 95014
(800) 752-0900

HHEA-Multimedia Systems
(Hitachi)
1290 Wall Street
West Lyndhurst, NJ 07071
(201) 935-5300 ext. 121

Infotek Inc.
56 Camille
E. Patchogue, NY 11772
(516) 289-9682

Lasertechnics, Inc.
5500 Wilshire Avenue NE
Albuquerque, NM 87113
(505) 821-2213

Linotype-Hell Company
425 Oser Avenue
Hauppauge, NY 11788
(800) 633-1900

Mannesmann Tally Corp.
8301 S. 180th Street
Kent, WA 98032
(800) 843-1347

Mitsubishi Electronics
America
5757 Plaza Drive
Cypress, CA 90630
(714) 220-2500

Mitsubishi International
Corp.
701 Westchester Avenue
White Plains, NY 10604
(914) 997-4999

NEC Technologies, Inc.
1414 Massachusetts Avenue
Boxborough, MA 01719
(800) 632-4636

Nikon Electronic Imaging
1300 Walt Whitman Road
Melville, NY 11747
(800) 526-4566

Oce Graphics USA, Inc.
385 Ravendale Drive
Mountain View, CA 94039-
7169
(800) 545-5445

Panasonic Communications
& Systems Co.
Two Panasonic Way
Secaucus, NJ 07094
(800) 742-8086

QMS Inc.
One Magnum Pass
Mobile, AL 36618
(800) 631-2692

Relax Technology, Inc.
3101 Whimple Road
Union City, CA 94587
(415) 471-6112

Sayett
100 Kings Hwy.
Rochester, NY 14617
(800) 836-7730

Seiko Instruments USA, Inc.
1130 Ringwood Court
San Jose, CA 95131
(800) 873-4561

Seikosha America, Inc.
10 Industrial Avenue
Mahwah, NJ 07430
(201) 327-7227

Sharp Electronics Corp.
One Sharp Plaza
Mahwah, NJ 07430
(201) 529-8200

Sony Corporation
Sony Drive
Park Ridge, NJ 07656
(201) 930-7796

Tektronix, Inc.
26600 SW Parkway
Wilsonville, OR 97070-1000
(800) 835-6100

Xerox Engineering Systems
Co.
2710 Walsh Avenue
Santa Clara, CA 95051
(408) 988-2800

Computer Projection Devices

3M Visual Systems Division
3M Austin Center
Bldg. A145-5N-01
Austin, TX 78769-9000
(800) 378-1371

Apollo Audio Visual
60 Trade Zone Court
Ronkonkoma, NY 11779
(516) 467-8033

Barco, Inc.
1000 Cobb Place Blvd.
Kennesaw, GA 30144
(404) 590-7900

Chisholm
910 Campisi Way
Campbell, CA 95008
(408) 559-0444

Dukane Corporation
Audio Visual Division
2900 Dukane Drive
St. Charles, IL 60174
(708) 584-2300

Eiki International
26794 Vista Terrace Drive
Lake Forest, CA 92630
(800) 242-3454

Electrohome Projection
Systems N.
809 Wellington Street
Kitchener, Ontario
Canada N2G 4J6
(800) 265-2171

Elmo Manufacturing
Corporation
70 New Hyde Park Road
New Hyde Park, NY 11040
(800) 654-7628

Esprit Projection Systems
AmPro Corporation
1301 Armstrong Drive
Titusville, FL 32780
(407) 269-6680

General Electric Company
Projection Display Products
Operation
Electronics Park 6-338
P.O. Box 4840
Syracuse, NY 13221
(315) 456-2152

Harman Video
8380 Balboa Blvd.
Northridge, CA 91360
(818) 893-9992

In Focus Systems, Inc.
7770 S.W. Mohawk Street
Tualatin, OR 97062
(800) 327-7231

Micronics Computers, Inc.
Portable Division
935 Benecia Avenue
Sunnyvale, CA 94086
(510) 651-2300

Mitsubshi Electronics America
5757 Plaza Drive
Cypress, CA 90630
(714) 220-2500

NEC Technologies, Inc.
1255 Michael Drive
Wood Dale, IL 60191
(708) 860-9500

nView
11835 Canon Blvd.
Newport News, VA 23606
(800) 736-8439

Panasonic Communication &
Systems Co.
One Panasonic Way
Secaucus, NJ 07014
(201) 392-6182

Proxima Corporation
6610 Nancy Ridge Drive
San Diego, CA 92121
(800) 447-7694

Pulsar Video Systems
7670 Clairemont Mesa Blvd.
San Diego, CA 92111
(800) 828-3811

Rever Computer, Inc.
18305 Valley Blvd., Suite H
La Puente, CA 91744
(818) 854-8768

Sanyo Industrial Video
1200 W. Artesia Blvd.
Compton, CA 90220
(310) 605-6527

Sayett Technology
17 Tobey Village Office Park
Pittsford, NY 14534
(716) 264-9250

Sharp Electronics Corporation
Sharp Plaza
Mahwah, NJ 07430
(201) 529-8731

Sony Business & Professional
Group
Projection System Marketing,
MDS 115
3 Paragon Drive
Montvale, NJ 07645
(201) 358-4191

Spectrel Corporation
1308 Bayshore Hwy.
Burlingame, CA 94010
(415) 343-5987

TDSD Corporation
9005 "A" Eton Avenue
Canoga Park, CA 91304
(818) 407-8991

Telex Communications, Inc.
9600 Aldrich Avenue S.
Minneapolis, MN 55420
(612) 884-4051

United Ventures, Inc.
4501 Route 13
Richmond, IL 60071
(815) 675-2277

VGT Corporation
P.O. 1039
Beaver, WV 25813
(304) 255-1194

Computer Projection Remote Controls

AMX Corporation
12056 Forestgate Drive
Dallas, TX 75243
(800) 222-0193

General Parametics Corp.
1250 9th Street
Berkeley, CA 94710
(800) 223-0999

Presentation Electronics, Inc.
3096 Wiese Way
Sacramento, CA 95833
(916) 646-3402

Film Recorders

Agfa Corporation
Compugraphic Division
1 Ramland Road
Orangeburg, NY 10962
(800) 227-2780

Autographix, Inc.
63 Third Avenue
Burlington, MA 01803
(617) 272-9000

Bell & Howell Quintar Co.
370 Amapola Avenue
Suite 106
Torrance, CA 90501-1475
(213) 320-5700

CELCO
70 Constantine Drive
Mahwah, NJ 07430
(201) 327-1123

Dicomed, Inc.
11401 Rupp Drive
Burnsville, MN 55337
(800) 888-7979

General Parametrics Corp.
1250 Ninth Street
Berkeley, CA 94710
(415) 524-3950

Lasergraphics
20 Ada
Irvine, CA 92718
(714) 727-2651

Management Graphics
1401 East 79th Street
Minneapolis, MN 55425
(612) 854-1220

NISE
20018 State Road
Cerritos, CA 90701
(213) 860-6708

Polaroid Corp.
549 Technology Square
Cambridge, MA 02139
(800) 225-1618

Presentation Technologies,
Inc.
779 Palomar Avenue
Sunnyvale, CA 94086
(800) 782-2543

Pointing Devices

Eastman Kodak Company
343 State Street
Rochester, NY 14650
(800) 344-0006

NAVITAR
200 Commerce Drive
Rochester, NY 14623
(800) 866-6362

Power Technology, Inc.
7925 Mabelvale Cutoff
Mabelvale, AR 72103
(501) 568-1995

Presentation Magazines

AVC Presentation Development & Delivery
445 Broad Hollow Road
Melville, NY 11747
(516) 845-2700

AVideo Production and Presentation Technology
Montage Publishing, Inc.
2550 Hawthorne Blvd.
Suite 314
Torrance, CA 90505
(213) 373-9993

Business Publishing
Hitchcock Publishing
191 S. Gary Avenue
Carol Stream, IL 60188
(708) 665-1000

Color Publishing/ Typeworld
PennWell Publishing Company
1421 South Sheridan
Tulsa, OK 74112
(508) 392-2157

Computer Graphics World
Circulation Dept. POB 122
Tulsa, OK 74101
(918) 831-9400

Computer Pictures
25550 Hawthorne Blvd.
Suite 314
Torrance, CA 90505
(213) 373-993

Computer Publishing Magazine
Pacific Magazine Group, Inc.
513 Wilshire Blvd., Ste. 344
Santa Monica, CA 90401
(213) 455-1414

Desktop Communications
P.O. Box 941745
Atlanta, GA 30341
(800) 966-9052

Instruction Delivery Systems
50 Culpeper Street
Warrenton, VA 22186
(703) 347-0055

Mac Publishing and Presentations
International Desktop
Communications Ltd.
530 Fifth Avenue
New York, NY 10036
(212) 768-7666

A number of publishers have accepted the challenge of publishing magazines for readers who want to enhance their learning and keep up with new developments in the area of presentations and computers.

New Media
901 Mariner's Island Blvd.
Suite 365
San Mateo, CA 94404
(415) 573-5170

PC Publishing and Presentations
International Desktop
Communications Ltd.
530 Fifth Avenue
New York, NY 10036
(212) 768-7666

Presentation Products Magazine
513 Wilshire Blvd., Suite 344
Santa Monica, CA 90401
(213) 455-1414

Publish
P.O. Box 55400
Boulder, CO 80322
(800) 274-5116

Special Resources

This section includes some of the authors' favorite resources that do not fit into any of the previous appendices. You may find several of them helpful in the creation and delivery of your presentations. Write or call for catalogs and/or information about services or products.

Graphix Zone
38 Corporate Park, Suite 100
Irvine, CA 92714
(714) 833-3838

Graphix Zone is a business developed on a completely new concept presenting everything you need to know about computer graphics and multimedia. It is a completely equipped facility where you can "test drive" the newest computer graphics and multimedia hardware and software in realistic settings. It is currently franchising and establishing centers throughout the United States.

IdeaFisher Systems, Inc.
18881 Von Karman Avenue
Ground Floor
Irvine, CA 92715
(800) 289-4332

Idea Fisher is a powerful new kind of interactive software for brainstorming and problem solving. It is a tool to help generate high-potential ideas and shape them in novel ways. A special module is available for helping you in developing presentation ideas.

Image Club Graphics

Suite 5, 1902 11 Street, S.E.
Calgary, Alberta T2G 3G2
Canada
(800) 661-9410

Image Club Graphics markets a wealth of clip art on either disk or CD-ROM. Its collection is very extensive and includes a wide variety of images that can be incorporated into your presentation visuals.

Interactive Color
A Guide for Color in Computer Graphics

Software Product Information
San Diego Supercomputer Center
P.O. Box 85608
San Diego, CA 92186-9784
(619) 534-5100

This software package is a unique interactive program on color concepts. The program is very informative on color and provides a good demonstration of interactive multimedia.

Minnesota Western Visual Presentation Systems

15405 Redhill Avenue, Suite E
Tustin, CA 92680-7301
(800) 999-8590

Minnesota Western Visual Presentation Systems provides a full range of presentation hardware, products, and supplies. The company has offices throughout California and Washington.

New Horizons Computer Learning Center

1231 E. Dyer Road, Suite 140
Santa Ana, CA 92705-5605
(714) 556-1220

This company provides excellent instruction–both in-house and on-site–on a wide variety of software. It is currently establishing franchises throughout the United States.

Paper Direct

205 Chubb Avenue
Lyndhurst, NJ 07071-0618
(800) 272–7377

Paper Direct provides a variety of unique types of paper for your handouts and brochures.

Visual Horizons

180 Metro Park
Rochester, NY 14623-2666
(716) 424-5300

This company provides a variety of presentation products and supplies.

Visualon

9000 Sweet Valley Drive
Cleveland, OH 44125
(216) 328-9000

Visualon provides a variety of presentation products, supplies, and equipment.

Index

About the Authors

The authors would like to share their teaching materials with you in case you find yourself instructing others on how to create high-impact presentations. For a slide package of 60 different 35mm slides or a packet of teaching materials including reading guides, sample course syllabi, learning measurements, and example presentations, write to:

Dr. Joyce Kupsh
21842 Harbor Breeze Lane
Huntington Beach, CA 92646

Dr. Joyce Kupsh is a professor in the College of Business Administration at California State Polytechnic University. Her doctoral work was completed at Arizona State University in the areas of business, education, and instructional technology. Presently, she teaches presentations and ergonomics at both the graduate and undergraduate levels and is director of the Presentation Design Center at Cal Poly State University.

Dr. Kupsh is a frequent speaker and has conducted seminars on a range of business topics throughout the United States and Canada. She is the author of five other books on business and design-related topics.

Dr. Pat R. Graves is an associate professor in the Department of Business Education and Administrative Information Systems at Eastern Illinois University. A recipient of the Lumpkin College of Business Distinguished Professor Award for her contributions in teaching, research, and service, she has also received a university-wide Faculty Excellence Award. Prior to joining Eastern Illinois University, Dr. Graves held positions on the faculties of the University of Kentucky and Memphis State University.

Dr. Graves is an active member of several professional organizations and is currently serving as Editor of the *Office Systems Research Journal.*